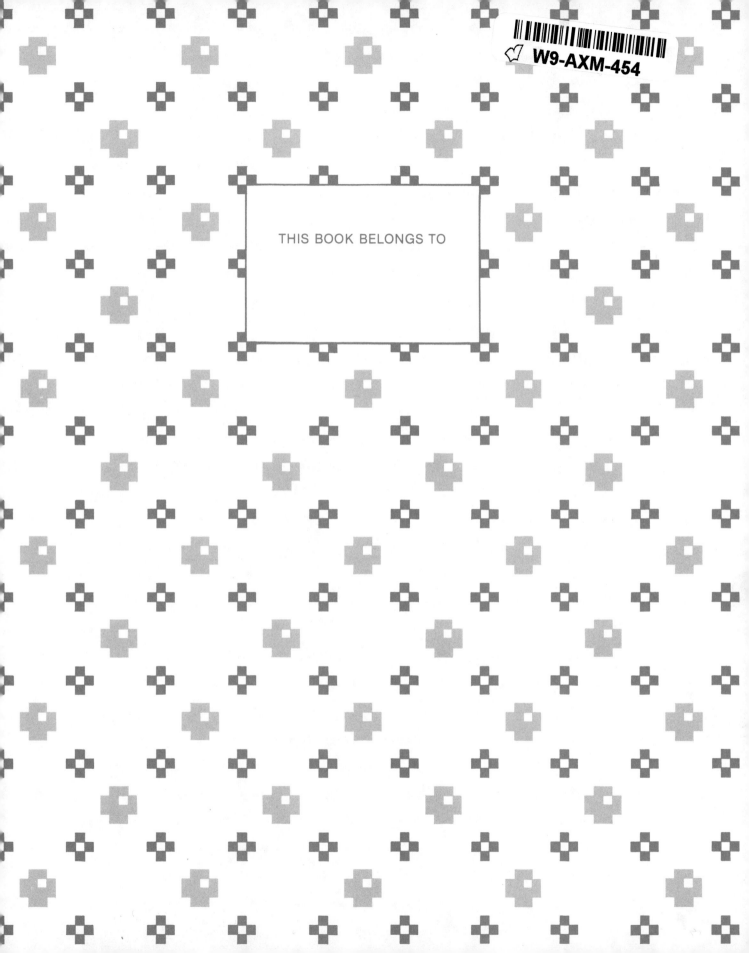

THIS BOOK BELONGS TO

Gifts of Love

Gifts of Love

by The Kooler Design Studio

Meredith® Press
New York, New York

Meredith® Press is an imprint of Meredith® Books;
President, Book Group: Joseph J. Ward
Vice-President, Editorial Director: Elizabeth P. Rice
For Meredith® Press
Executive Editor: Maryanne Bannon
Associate Editor: Carolyn Mitchell
Production Manager: Bill Rose

For Chapelle Limited
Owner: Jo Packham
Staff: Trice Boerens, Gaylene Byers, Holly Fuller, Cherie Hanson, Susan Jorgensen, Margaret Shields Marti, Jackie McCowen, Barbara Millburn, Pamela Randall, Jennifer Roberts, Florence Stacey, Nancy Whitley and Lorrie Young

Photographer: Ryne Hazen

The photographs in this book were taken at the home of Jo Packham.

ISBN: 0-696-02394-6
Library of Congress: 93-077502
First Printing 1993

Distributed by Meredith Corporation, Des Moines, IA.

10 9 8 7 6 5 4 3 2 1

Printed in the United States of America.

Dear Cross-Stitcher,

Gifts of Love is Donna Kooler's second book for Meredith® Press. A well known designer of cross-stitch kits and leaflets, she now combines her talents with the unmistakable style of The Vanessa-Ann Collection.

This volume contains the varied and interesting project ideas and techniques that cross-stitchers demand. Choose from large framed samplers or small derivative pieces, soft or intense colors, vintage or contemporary designs.

As in all Meredith® Press books, each project is paired with concise directions and an illustrative color photo. We've tried to ensure that design charts are clearly rendered with shading and symbols. A glossary and full chapter of general information keep you covered from stitch to stitch. You'll also find a helpful supplier page listing sources for canvases and floss.

We present *Gifts of Love* with the simple intent—in Donna's words—to make your life more beautiful.

Sincerely,

Maryanne Bannon

Maryanne Bannon
Executive Editor

Crisp white walls, tall arched windows, framed needlework designs displayed everywhere and a long rainbow-colored yarn wall form the backdrop for Kooler Design Studio, Inc., in Martinez, California. It's a setting that encourages creativity and the Kooler team is indeed that! But what makes this studio unique are the people who work in and inhabit this wonderful setting.

Eight years ago Donna Kooler gathered a group of people together and started a design studio. Over the next few years it began to grow and Donna's supportive management style enabled the group to become a close-knit team. Her encouragement and assistance in trying new and innovative things, as well as the home-away-from-home setting, seem to be the secret ingredient for the esprit de corps.

The staff now consists of art needlework designers Linda Gillum, Nancy Rossi, Barbara Baatz, Jorja Hernandez and Holly DeFount. Priscilla Timm designs exclusively for plastic canvas and supervises the in-house stitchers. Loretta Heden is the text writer and manages the office and Janet Hanner is the stylist. Professional in-house stitchers and painters Sara Angle, Anita Forfang, Virginia Hanley-Rivett, Vivian Harlin, Marsha Hinkson, Arlis Johnson, Veronkia Maines, Michele O'Conner, Lori Patton, Charlyce Randolph and Giana Tarricone complete the team. They take the designs from a concept and create a work of art. In addition to these people, a large group of free-lance designers works with the studio, and some of them contributed to this book, the second American Sampler by the Kooler Design Studios. They are Lori Birmingham, Ruth Houseworth, Lorna McRoden and April Vegas.

It is the hope of all those at the Kooler Design Studio that you enjoy these pieces and that they add that special personal touch to your home. It is their wish to pass on to you feelings of warmth, caring and "family."

*When love
and skill
come together,
expect a
masterpiece*

—

Unknown

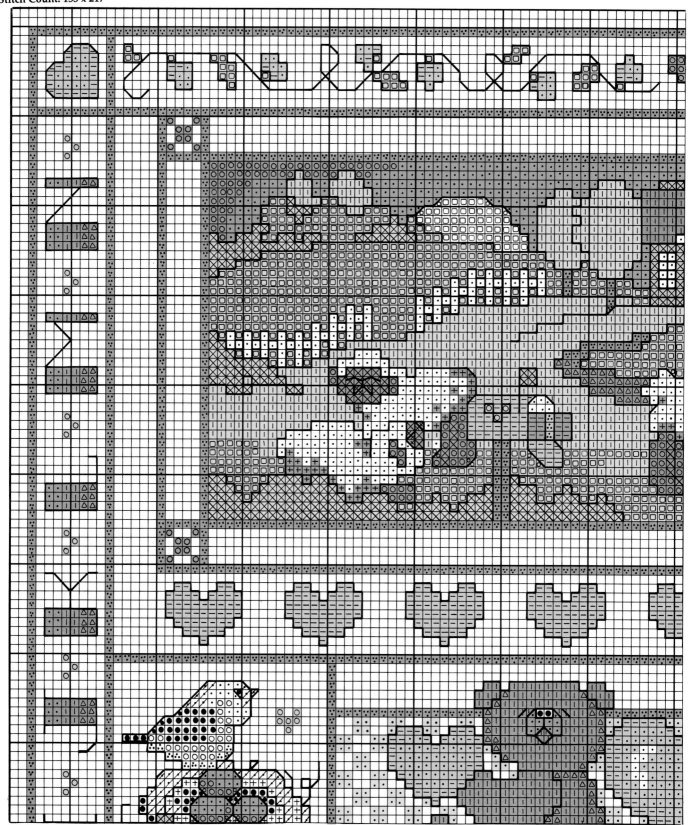

10

11

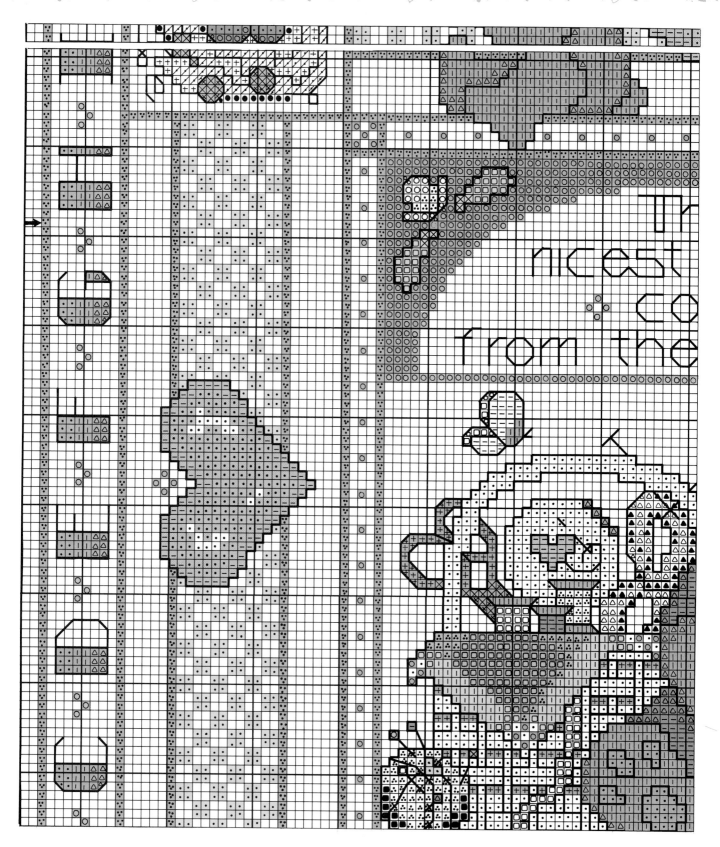

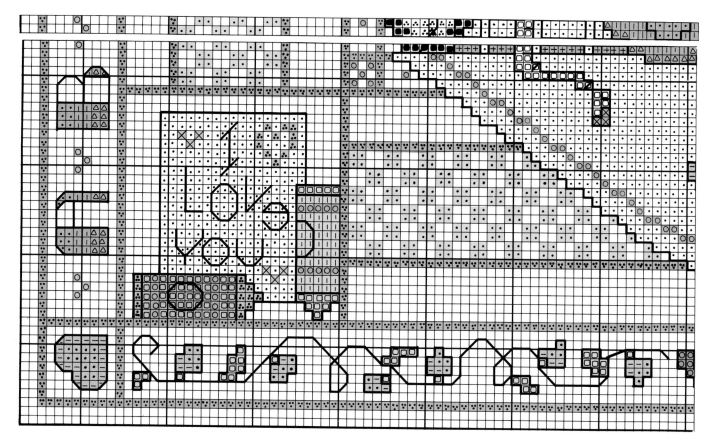

The Nicest Gifts

Stitched on cream Linen 28 over 2 threads, the finished design size is 10⅞" x 15½". The fabric was cut 17" x 22".

FABRICS   **DESIGN SIZES**
Aida 11   13⅞" x 19¾"
Aida 14   10⅞" x 15½"
Aida 18   8½" x 12"
Hardanger 22   7" x 9⅞"

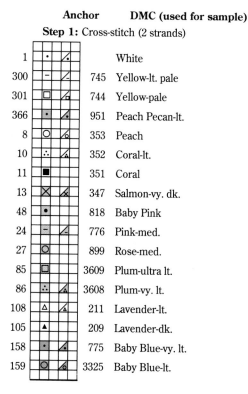

Anchor			DMC	(used for sample)

Step 1: Cross-stitch (2 strands)

Anchor		DMC	Color
1			White
300		745	Yellow-lt. pale
301		744	Yellow-pale
366		951	Peach Pecan-lt.
8		353	Peach
10		352	Coral-lt.
11		351	Coral
13		347	Salmon-vy. dk.
48		818	Baby Pink
24		776	Pink-med.
27		899	Rose-med.
85		3609	Plum-ultra lt.
86		3608	Plum-vy. lt.
108		211	Lavender-lt.
105		209	Lavender-dk.
158		775	Baby Blue-vy. lt.
159		3325	Baby Blue-lt.

14

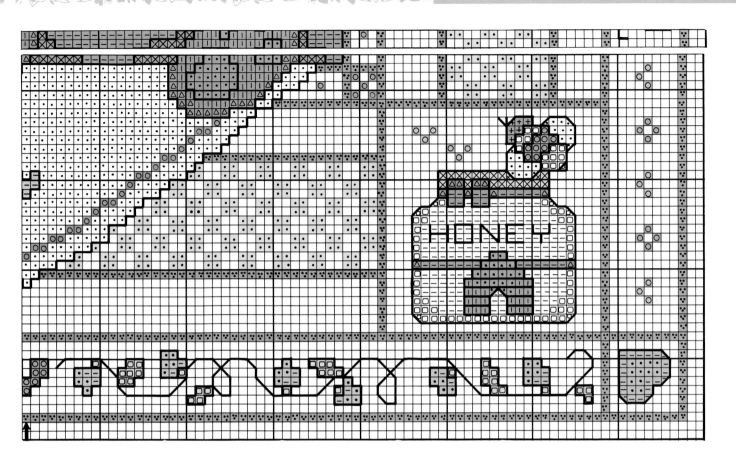

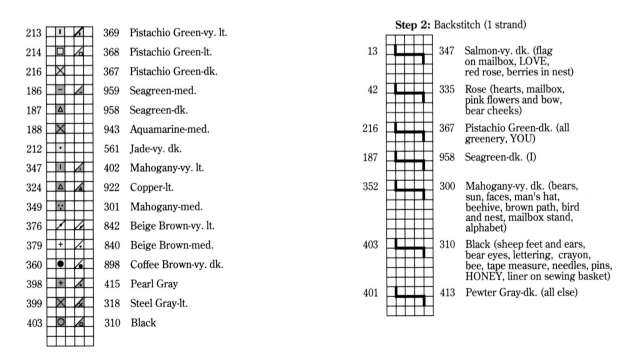

			369	Pistachio Green-vy. lt.
213	I	◪	369	Pistachio Green-vy. lt.
214	□	◪	368	Pistachio Green-lt.
216	✕		367	Pistachio Green-dk.
186	–	◪	959	Seagreen-med.
187	△		958	Seagreen-dk.
188	✕		943	Aquamarine-med.
212	•		561	Jade-vy. dk.
347	I	◪	402	Mahogany-vy. lt.
324	△	◪	922	Copper-lt.
349	⦙		301	Mahogany-med.
376	╱	◪	842	Beige Brown-vy. lt.
379	+	◪	840	Beige Brown-med.
360	●	◪	898	Coffee Brown-vy. dk.
398	+	◪	415	Pearl Gray
399	✕	◪	318	Steel Gray-lt.
403	○	◪	310	Black

Step 2: Backstitch (1 strand)

13		347	Salmon-vy. dk. (flag on mailbox, LOVE, red rose, berries in nest)
42		335	Rose (hearts, mailbox, pink flowers and bow, bear cheeks)
216		367	Pistachio Green-dk. (all greenery, YOU)
187		958	Seagreen-dk. (I)
352		300	Mahogany-vy. dk. (bears, sun, faces, man's hat, beehive, brown path, bird and nest, mailbox stand, alphabet)
403		310	Black (sheep feet and ears, bear eyes, lettering, crayon, bee, tape measure, needles, pins, HONEY, liner on sewing basket)
401		413	Pewter Gray-dk. (all else)

Honey Bear

Heart: Stitched on white Belfast Linen 32 over 2 threads, the finished design size is ½" x ⅜". The fabric was cut 6" x 6".

FABRICS	DESIGN SIZES
Aida 11	⅞" x ⅝"
Aida 14	⅝" x ½"
Aida 18	½" x ⅜"
Hardanger 22	⅜" x ⅜"

Stitch Count: 9 x 7

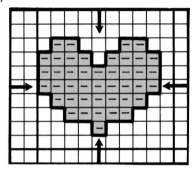

Honey bee: Stitched on white Belfast Linen 32 over 2 threads, the finished design size is 1⅛" x 1⅜". The fabric was cut 9" x 4".

FABRICS	DESIGN SIZES
Aida 11	1¾" x 2⅛"
Aida 14	1⅜" x 1⅝"
Aida 18	1" x 1¼"
Hardanger 22	⅞" x 1"

Stitch Count: 19 x 23

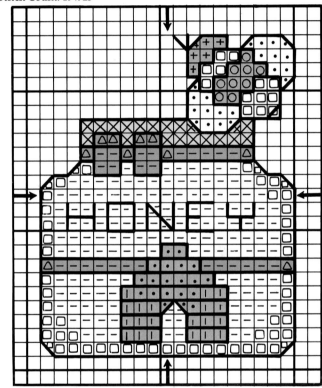

Step 2: Backstitch (1 strand)

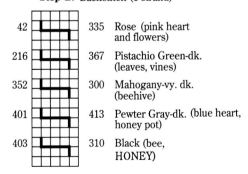

	335	Rose (pink heart and flowers)
42		
216	367	Pistachio Green-dk. (leaves, vines)
352	300	Mahogany-vy. dk. (beehive)
401	413	Pewter Gray-dk. (blue heart, honey pot)
403	310	Black (bee, HONEY)

Anchor   DMC (used for sample)

Step 1: Cross-stitch (2 strands)

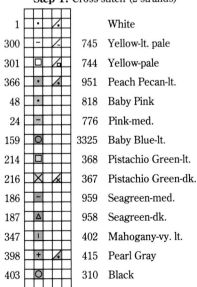

Anchor	DMC	
1		White
300	745	Yellow-lt. pale
301	744	Yellow-pale
366	951	Peach Pecan-lt.
48	818	Baby Pink
24	776	Pink-med.
159	3325	Baby Blue-lt.
214	368	Pistachio Green-lt.
216	367	Pistachio Green-dk.
186	959	Seagreen-med.
187	958	Seagreen-dk.
347	402	Mahogany-vy. lt.
398	415	Pearl Gray
403	310	Black

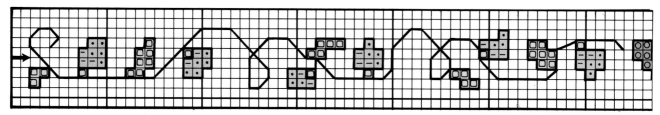

Stitch Count: 131 x 6

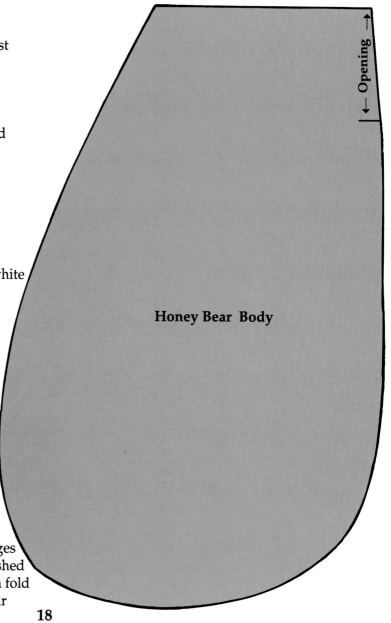

Honey Bear Body

Flower border: Stitched on white Belfast Linen 32 over 2 threads, the finished design size is 8⅛" x ⅜". The fabric was cut 12" x 8". Begin stitching border 2" above center of bottom 12" edge.

MATERIALS

Three completed design pieces on white Belfast Linen 32; matching thread
4" square of unstitched white Belfast Linen 32
⅜ yard of blue-and-white pin-striped fabric; matching thread
¼ yard of tan polished cotton; matching thread
⅜ yard of white cotton
¼ yard of fleece
⅝ yard of ½"-wide white lace trim
¾ yard of ¼"-wide white satin ribbon
¾ yard of ⅛"-wide elastic
12" of 18-gauge craft wire
4"-long ½"-wide dowel
Acrylic paints: tan, dark brown, pink, black, white
Paintbrush
Liquid ravel preventer
Sculpey III modeling compound
Gesso
Matte finish spray
1¾"-tall miniature wooden bucket with a 2¼" circumference and removable wire handle
Large-eyed needle
Polyester stuffing
Tracing paper
Dressmaker's pen
Needle-nose pliers

DIRECTIONS

1. Make patterns for bear and bear clothes (pages 18– 21, transferring all information. From polished cotton, cut two body pieces, two arm pieces on fold and four leg pieces. From white cotton, cut four

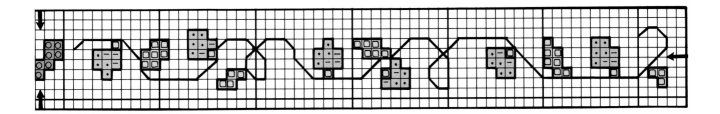

bloomer pieces. From pin-striped fabric, cut dress front on fold, two dress backs, two 5" x 7" pieces for sleeves and one 7" x 24" piece for skirt. With design centered, cut one pinafore bib for front from heart design piece. From unstitched linen, cut one pinafore bib for lining. From floral design piece, cut one 5" x 9" piece for pinafore skirt, centering design 1½" above one long edge. Apply liquid ravel preventer to edges of linen pieces to prevent fraying.

2. Make head. Using modeling compound, mold head according to Diagrams A and B. Insert dowel at base of head. Mold neck around dowel to 2" in

length. Remove dowel. Bake according to manufacturer's instructions. Allow to dry until hard. Paint head tan. Allow to dry. Paint cheeks and inner ears pink. Paint nose and mouth black; paint eyes as desired. Allow to dry. Spray bear head with matte finish. To prime feet, paint with gesso. Transfer shoes from leg pattern to bear feet. Paint shoes black. Allow to dry.

3. Make bear. With right sides facing, stitch body pieces, leaving top open and an opening in back according to pattern. Fold neckline ½" to wrong side of fabric. Sew gathering stitches around

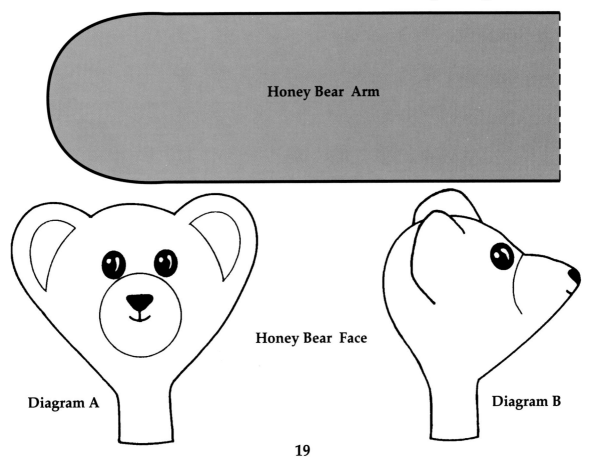

Honey Bear Arm

Honey Bear Face

Diagram A

Diagram B

neckline close to fold. Turn. With right sides facing, stitch two leg pieces together, leaving an opening in back according to pattern. Repeat. Turn legs. Place legs on opposite sides of body 1" from bottom. Stitch legs together through body. Stuff legs firmly. Slipstitch openings closed. With right sides facing, stitch two arm pieces together, leaving an opening according to pattern. Turn. Using needle-nose pliers, make a ½"-long hook on each end of craft wire. Insert wire into opening in arms. Stuff moderately, except in center of length. Slipstitch opening closed. Center arms horizontally on bear back 1½" below neckline. Bend arms into desired shape. Tack to bear back. Stuff body. Slipstitch opening in bear back closed. Insert neck into body 1½". Gather neckline tightly around neck. Secure.

4. Make bloomers. With right sides facing, stitch bloomers center front and back seams. Fold bloomer top ¼" double to wrong side of fabric. Stitch close to first folded edge through all layers, leaving an opening. From elastic, cut one 7½" length and two 4" lengths. Thread 7½" length through casing. Stitch opening closed. From lace trim, cut two 7" lengths; set remaining lace trim aside. Stitch one 7" length around bottom of each bloomer leg. Fold ½" to wrong side on each lower leg. Zigzag one elastic length on raw edge,

securing ends of elastic and gathering fabric. Repeat. With right sides facing, stitch inseam, securing lace and elastic ends.

5. Make dress. With right sides facing, stitch one bodice back to bodice front at shoulder seams. Repeat. Sew gathering stitches on one 7" edge of each sleeve. With right sides facing, pin one sleeve to each side of bodice, matching center of gathered edge to shoulder seam. Fold sleeve ends ¼" double to wrong side of fabric. Stitch close to first folded edge through all layers, leaving an opening. From elastic, cut two 4" lengths. Thread elastic through casing. Stitch opening closed. Stitch along sleeve and side seam securing elastic. Repeat. With right sides facing, fold skirt so that short edges meet; stitch. Sew gathering stitches along one long edge. Stitch gathered edge of skirt to bodice bottom edge. Hem dress ¾". Stitch remaining lace trim to neckline. Slide dress on bear. Slipstitch back opening closed.

6. Make pinafore. From ribbon, cut two 3½" lengths and one 20" length. With right sides facing and raw edges aligned, pin one small ribbon length to each shoulder of bib front. With right sides facing, stitch bib front to lining along top, side seams and shoulder seams, securing ribbon ends in seam.

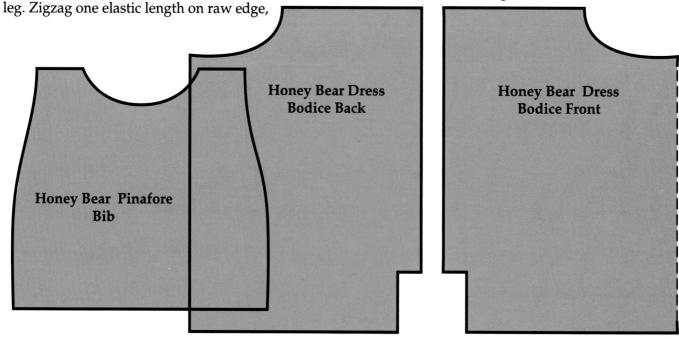

Honey Bear Pinafore Bib

Honey Bear Dress Bodice Back

Honey Bear Dress Bodice Front

Turn. Sew gathering stitches along edge of pinafore skirt opposite floral design. Center gathered edge of skirt below stitched bib. With gathered edge of skirt and bottom edge of bib aligned, stitch skirt to bib. Center long ribbon length on right side of bib front on bottom edge. Stitch ribbon to bib, leaving matching ends. Stitch ends of 3½" ribbon lengths to long ribbon length. Slip pinafore on bear. Tie ribbon in bow.

7. Make bucket. Paint bucket interior and exterior brown. Allow to dry. Center and pin fleece to wrong side of honey bee design piece. With right sides facing, fold design piece so that long edges meet. Stitch. Turn. Remove handle from bucket. Slide band onto bucket. Fold one end under ¼". Slide second end inside folded end. Slipstitch securely. Using large-eyed needle, make holes in design piece to insert bucket handle. Replace bucket handle.

1 square = 1 inch

Center Front/Back

Honey Bear Bloomers

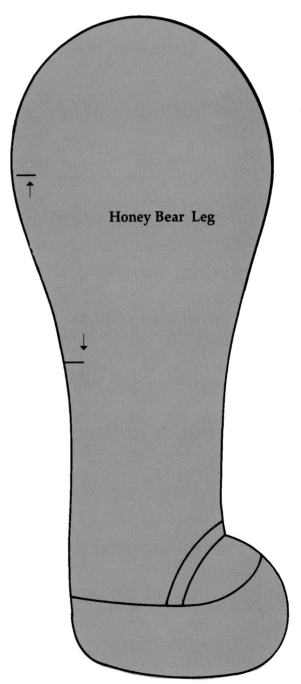

Honey Bear Leg

*Nature
is man's
religious book,
with lessons
for every day.*

—

Theodore Parker

Nature's Gifts

Stitched on natural Linen 28 over 2 threads, the finished design size is 9⅛" x 10¾". The fabric was cut 16" x 17".

FABRICS	DESIGN SIZES
Aida 11	11½" x 13¾"
Aida 14	9⅛" x 10¾"
Aida 18	7" x 8⅜"
Hardanger 22	5¾" x 6⅞"

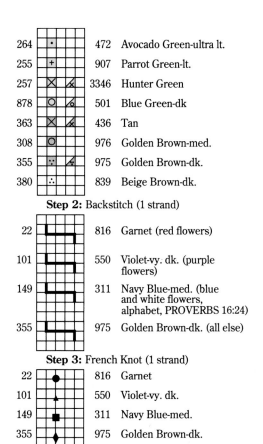

Anchor   DMC (used for sample)

Step 1: Cross-stitch (2 strands)

Anchor	DMC	Color
1		White
886	677	Old Gold-vy. lt.
891	676	Old Gold-lt.
894	223	Shell Pink-med.
74	3354	Dusty Rose-vy. lt.
22	816	Garnet
108	211	Lavender-lt.
98	553	Violet-med.
101	550	Violet-vy. dk.
158	775	Baby Blue-vy. lt.
921	931	Antique Blue-med.
147	312	Navy Blue-lt.
149	311	Navy Blue-med.

Anchor	DMC	Color
264	472	Avocado Green-ultra lt.
255	907	Parrot Green-lt.
257	3346	Hunter Green
878	501	Blue Green-dk.
363	436	Tan
308	976	Golden Brown-med.
355	975	Golden Brown-dk.
380	839	Beige Brown-dk.

Step 2: Backstitch (1 strand)

Anchor	DMC	Color
22	816	Garnet (red flowers)
101	550	Violet-vy. dk. (purple flowers)
149	311	Navy Blue-med. (blue and white flowers, alphabet, PROVERBS 16:24)
355	975	Golden Brown-dk. (all else)

Step 3: French Knot (1 strand)

Anchor	DMC	Color
22	816	Garnet
101	550	Violet-vy. dk.
149	311	Navy Blue-med.
355	975	Golden Brown-dk.

Flowers at Your Fingertips

Stitched on Quaker Cloth 28 over 2 threads, the finished design size for one repeat is 3½" x 3½". The flower border was repeated six times. The fabric was cut 24" x 28".

FABRICS	DESIGN SIZES
Aida 11	4½" x 4½"
Aida 14	3½" x 3½"
Aida 18	2¾" x 2¾"
Hardanger 22	2¼" x 2¼"

MATERIALS

Completed design piece on Quaker Cloth; matching thread
1¼ yards of ⅛"-wide blue ribbon
Matching embroidery floss

DIRECTIONS

1. With design centered horizontally, cut the fabric to 21½" x 27½".

2. Fold top and side edges ¼" double to wrong side and hem by hand; leave bottom edge unstitched.

3. Draw one ⅛"-wide row of threads for hemstitching ⅜" from top of design. Repeat ⅜" below design.

4. Fold bottom edge of fabric under ½"; then fold again to align with bottom edge of drawn threads for hemstitching. Baste in place.

5. Ladder hemstitch both rows of drawn threads; see general instructions on page 142. Weave ribbon into hemstitching, allowing 1½" on each end to weave into back. Secure ribbons at hemmed sides.

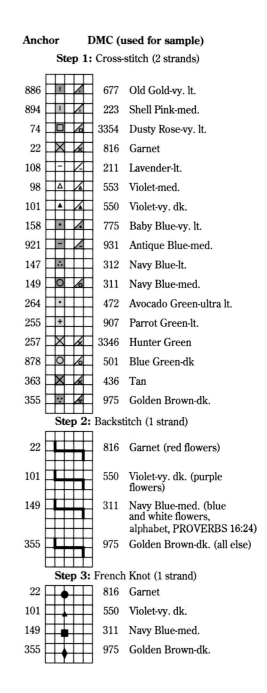

Anchor		DMC (used for sample)	
Step 1: Cross-stitch (2 strands)			
886		677	Old Gold-vy. lt.
894		223	Shell Pink-med.
74		3354	Dusty Rose-vy. lt.
22		816	Garnet
108		211	Lavender-lt.
98		553	Violet-med.
101		550	Violet-vy. dk.
158		775	Baby Blue-vy. lt.
921		931	Antique Blue-med.
147		312	Navy Blue-lt.
149		311	Navy Blue-med.
264		472	Avocado Green-ultra lt.
255		907	Parrot Green-lt.
257		3346	Hunter Green
878		501	Blue Green-dk.
363		436	Tan
355		975	Golden Brown-dk.
Step 2: Backstitch (1 strand)			
22		816	Garnet (red flowers)
101		550	Violet-vy. dk. (purple flowers)
149		311	Navy Blue-med. (blue and white flowers, alphabet, PROVERBS 16:24)
355		975	Golden Brown-dk. (all else)
Step 3: French Knot (1 strand)			
22		816	Garnet
101		550	Violet-vy. dk.
149		311	Navy Blue-med.
355		975	Golden Brown-dk.

Stitch Count: 49 x 17

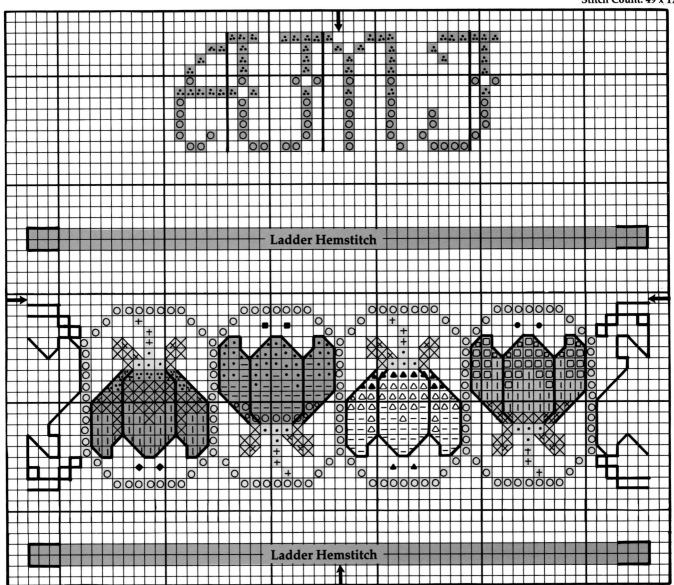

"A Bee C" Tissue Box

Stitched on 3"-wide band of natural Linen 28 with hemstitched border over 2 threads, the finished design size is 18⅞" x 1⅛". The fabric was cut 24" long.

FABRICS	DESIGN SIZES
Aida 11	24" x 1½"
Aida 14	18 ⅞" x 1⅛"
Aida 18	14 ⅝" x ⅞"
Hardanger 22	12" x ¾"

MATERIALS

Completed design piece on natural Linen; matching thread
¼ yard of blue fabric; matching thread
Plastic tissue box cover: 6" high x 5" wide
1¼ yards of ⅛"-wide blue ribbon
Fleece
Hot glue gun and glue sticks

Anchor		DMC (used for sample)	
Step 1: Cross-stitch (2 strands)			
1			White
891		676	Old Gold-lt.
147		312	Navy Blue-lt.
149		311	Navy Blue-med.
255		907	Parrot Green-lt.
878		501	Blue Green-dk.
363		436	Tan
Step 2: Backstitch (1 strand)			
149		311	Navy Blue-med. (alphabet, flowers)
355		975	Golden Brown-dk. (bee)

DIRECTIONS
All seams are ¼".

1. Cut fabric into a 21" x 11" strip. Cut fleece into a 20½" x 7" strip.

2. Align long edge of fleece with bottom edge of tissue box cover. Glue, trimming excess from one end as needed. Wrap fleece into top opening, dispersing fullness evenly. Run a bead of glue around inside edge of opening. Wet fingers slightly and quickly fold fleece over glue and hold until secure. (The water on your hands resists the hot glue and keeps you from being burned.) Trim excess fleece.

3. With right sides facing, stitch short ends of fabric strip together. Right side out, slide fabric over tissue box cover, placing seam at one corner. (The fabric should fit smoothly but not tightly.) Follow process used with fleece above to finish top opening, gluing fabric beyond edge of fleece to tissue box cover itself. With fabric smooth, fold remaining fabric inside bottom opening. Glue in place.

4. Weave ribbon into hemstitching on design piece. Wrap design piece around tissue box cover; see photo. Pin in place. Fold one short edge under and overlap at back of tissue box cover. Slipstitch edges together; remove pins. Secure with additional glue.

Blossoming Basket

Stitched on 3"-wide band of natural Linen 28 with hemstitched border over 2 threads, the finished design size for one repeat is 3½" x 1¼". The flower border is taken from the towel graph on page 31. Cut the fabric 37" long or to fit your wastebasket.

FABRICS	DESIGN SIZES
Aida 11	4½" x 1½"
Aida 14	3½" x 1¼"
Aida 18	2¾" x 1
Hardanger 22	2¼" x ¾"

MATERIALS

Completed design piece on natural Linen; matching thread
1 yard of blue fabric
Blue plastic wastebasket: 10" high x 7" wide
2 yards of ⅛"-wide blue ribbon
Fleece
1 yard of narrow elastic
Hot glue gun and glue sticks

DIRECTIONS

1. Cut fabric into a 27" x 30" piece. Cut fleece into a 27" x 30" piece.

2. Center bottom of wastebasket over fleece. Tie elastic around top of wastebasket about 1" from top edge so that it fits snugly. Wrap fleece around wastebasket, tucking under elastic and folding excess to corners. Trim fleece ½" from top edge of wastebasket and glue edge in place. Trim excess from corners and glue edges as needed.

3. Place fabric wrong side up on flat surface, center wastebasket bottom on it. Wrap fabric around wastebasket, tucking under elastic. Pull fabric slightly to make smooth and disperse fullness evenly around top edge. Trim fabric even with top edge of wastebasket and glue edge securely in place. Remove elastic.

4. Weave ribbon into hemstitching on design piece. Wrap design piece around top of wastebasket, covering raw edges of fabric. Pin in place. Fold one short edge under and overlap at back of wastebasket. Slipstitch edges together; remove pins.

Life is a flame that is always burning itself out, but it catches fire again every time a child is born.

—

George Bernard Shaw

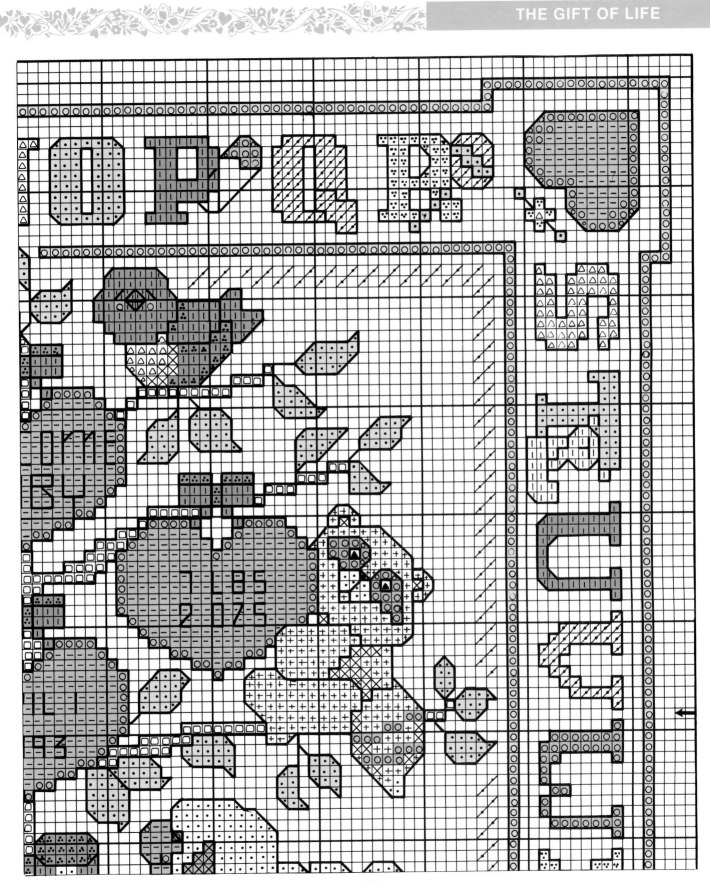

The Gift of Life

Stitched on white Aida 14 over 1 thread, the finished design size is 8⅞" x 8⅜". The fabric was cut 15" x 15".

FABRICS	DESIGN SIZES
Aida 11	11¼" x 10⅝"
Aida 18	6⅞" x 6½"
Hardanger 22	5⅝" x 5⅜"

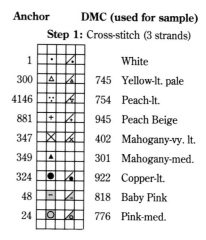

Anchor			DMC (used for sample)	
			Step 1: Cross-stitch (3 strands)	
1				White
300			745	Yellow-lt. pale
4146			754	Peach-lt.
881			945	Peach Beige
347			402	Mahogany-vy. lt.
349			301	Mahogany-med.
324			922	Copper-lt.
48			818	Baby Pink
24			776	Pink-med.

38

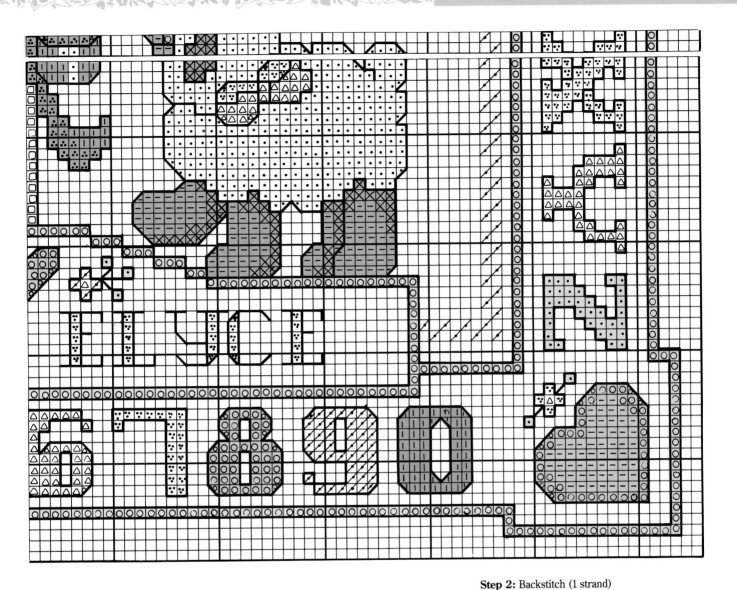

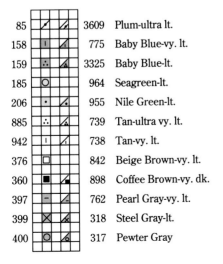

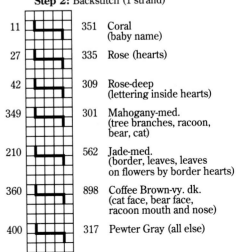

85			3609	Plum-ultra lt.
158			775	Baby Blue-vy. lt.
159			3325	Baby Blue-lt.
185			964	Seagreen-lt.
206			955	Nile Green-lt.
885			739	Tan-ultra vy. lt.
942			738	Tan-vy. lt.
376			842	Beige Brown-vy. lt.
360			898	Coffee Brown-vy. dk.
397			762	Pearl Gray-vy. lt.
399			318	Steel Gray-lt.
400			317	Pewter Gray

Step 2: Backstitch (1 strand)

11		351	Coral (baby name)
27		335	Rose (hearts)
42		309	Rose-deep (lettering inside hearts)
349		301	Mahogany-med. (tree branches, racoon, bear, cat)
210		562	Jade-med. (border, leaves, leaves on flowers by border hearts)
360		898	Coffee Brown-vy. dk. (cat face, bear face, racoon mouth and nose)
400		317	Pewter Gray (all else)

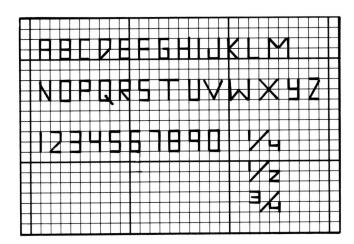

Cuddly Kitty

Stitched with Waste Canvas 14 over pink fabric, the finished bird motif size is 2⅞" x 1¼". The pink fabric was cut 4½" x 15". Begin stitching 4½" from short edge of fabric with bottom edge of design 1¼" from bottom long edge of fabric. Repeat border stitches along length of fabric.

MATERIALS

Completed design piece on pink fabric; matching thread
¼ yard of muslin; matching thread
⅛ yard of floral fabric; matching thread
⅛ yard of unstitched pink fabric; matching thread
⅛ yard of white fabric; matching thread
¼ yard of ½"-wide white lace trim
1 yard of ⅛"-wide elastic
Two bow-shaped buttons
Polyester stuffing
Tracing paper
Dressmaker's pen
Gesso
Acrylic paints: yellow, brown, green, pink, white, black
Paintbrushes
Hot glue gun and glue sticks

DIRECTIONS

All seams are ¼". All elastic lengths include 2" of excess for ease in handling.

1. Make pattern for cat and cat clothes (pages 45–47). From muslin, cut two body pieces and four legs. From floral fabric, cut shirt front on fold and two shirt backs. From white fabric, cut two bloomer pieces.

2. With right sides facing, stitch body pieces, leaving bottom open. Turn. Stuff firmly. With right sides facing, stitch two legs, leaving top open. Repeat. Turn legs. Stuff firmly. Insert legs ½" into body. Slipstitch body closed, catching legs in seam.

3. To prime fabric for painting, apply gesso to cat head, hands and feet. Allow to dry. Paint primed areas yellow. Allow to dry. Paint brown markings on face, hands and feet as desired. Allow to dry. Transfer facial features to cat. Paint eyes green; nose, mouth and inner ears pink. Outline all else with black and paint pupils black. Accent pupils with white.

4. With right sides facing, stitch shirt back to front at shoulder seam and along sleeve top. Repeat. Fold sleeve ends ½" to wrong side of fabric and stitch ¼" from folded edge. From elastic, cut two 4½" lengths. Thread elastic into casing. Pull elastic to gather sleeve end to 2½". Stitch shirt side seams and along sleeve underside, catching elastic in seam. Trim excess. Fold neckline ½" to wrong side of fabric and stitch ¼" from folded edge. From elastic, cut one 5" piece. Thread elastic into casing. Turn shirt. Hem bottom edge ½". Slide onto cat. Pull excess elastic to gather shirt around cat neck. Knot elastic ends; trim excess. Slipstitch shirt back closed.

5. With right sides facing, stitch bloomer side seams. Fold bloomer top and each leg bottom ½" to wrong side of fabric. From elastic, cut two 5" pieces and one 7" piece. Thread short pieces of elastic into casing in legs. Pull excess to gather fabric to 3". Repeat with long piece of elastic and bloomer top, gathering top to 5". Stitch opening closed, catching elastic in seam. Trim excess. Cut trim into two equal lengths. Stitch trim ½" from bottom of each bloomer leg. Stitch bloomers inseam. Turn. Slide bloomers on cat.

6. To make jumper, fold design piece, right sides facing, so that short ends meet. Stitch along short edges. With seam centered in back, flatten design piece into a tube. Press folds. To make arm holes, cut a 2" semicircle from the top of each fold; see Diagram. Fold jumper top ½" to wrong side of fabric. Sew gathering stitches close to fold. To make straps, cut two ¾" x 3½" pieces from unstitched pink fabric. With wrong sides facing, fold in half so that long edges meet; stitch. Stitch straps to jumper. Turn jumper. Hem ½". Put jumper on cat. Sew buttons to front at strap ends.

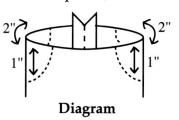

Diagram

Stitch Count: 41 x 18

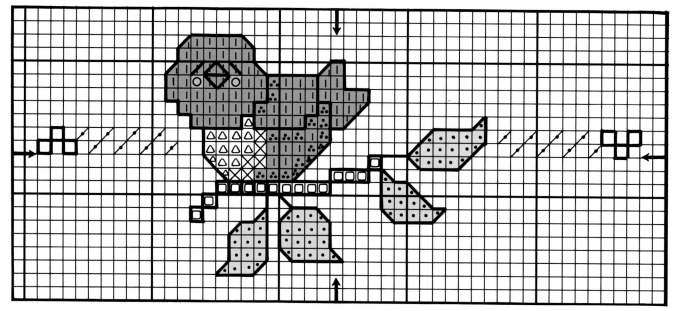

42

Stitch Count: 10 x 30

Precious Pup

Stitched with Waste Canvas 14 over blue fabric, the finished design size is ¾" x 2⅛". The blue fabric was cut 6" x 8". Begin stitching top "B" ½" from right edge and 3" from bottom edge of fabric. To personalize the lettering, replace these letters with desired letters from sampler on pages 36-39.

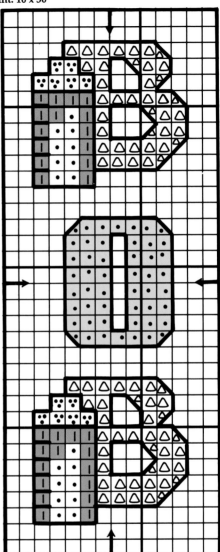

FABRICS	DESIGN SIZES
Aida 11	⅞" x 2¾"
Aida 18	½" x 1⅝"
Hardanger 22	½" x 1⅜"

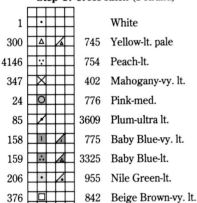

Anchor		DMC (used for sample)	
Step 1: Cross-stitch (1 strand)			
1			White
300		745	Yellow-lt. pale
4146		754	Peach-lt.
347		402	Mahogany-vy. lt.
24		776	Pink-med.
85		3609	Plum-ultra lt.
158		775	Baby Blue-vy. lt.
159		3325	Baby Blue-lt.
206		955	Nile Green-lt.
376		842	Beige Brown-vy. lt.

Step 2: Backstitch (1 strand)			
349		301	Mahogany-med. (tree branch)
210		562	Jade-med. (leaves)
400		317	Pewter Gray (all else)

MATERIALS

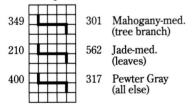

Completed design piece on blue fabric; matching thread
¼ yard of muslin; matching thread
¼ yard of unstitched blue fabric
⅛ yard of yellow fabric; matching thread
⅛ yard of white fabric; matching thread
5" square of blue-and-white striped fabric
Two car-shaped buttons

Tracing paper
Dressmaker's pen
Polyester stuffing
Gesso
Acrylic paints: gray, pink, white, black
Paintbrushes
Hot glue gun and glue sticks

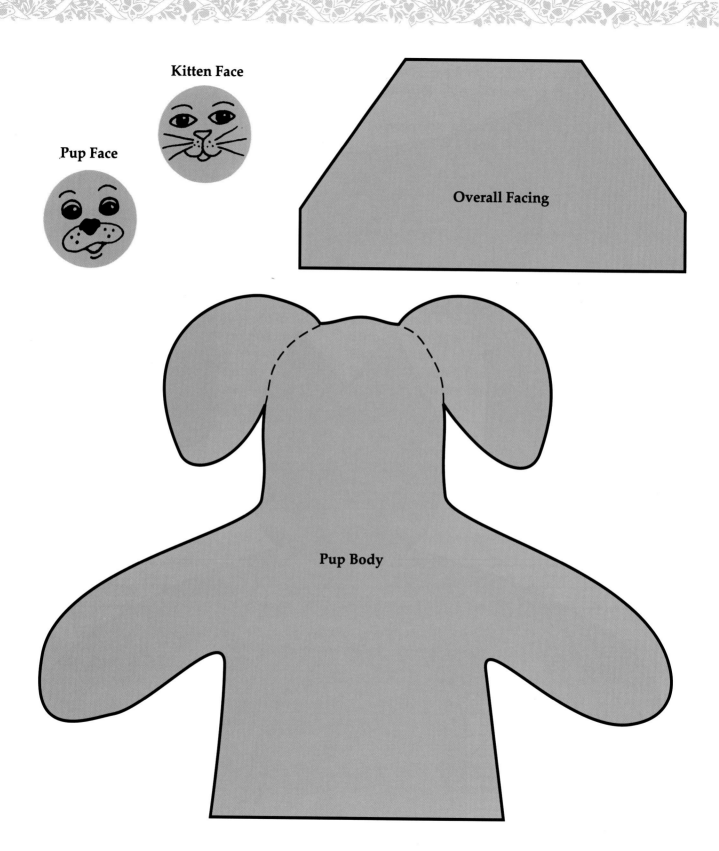

Kitten Face

Pup Face

Overall Facing

Pup Body

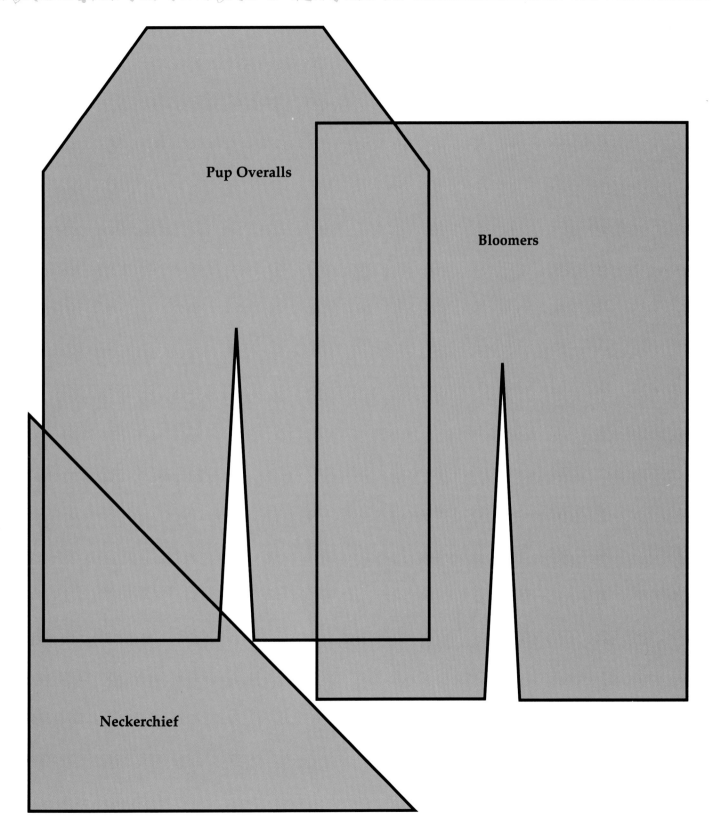

Pup Overalls

Bloomers

Neckerchief

*Pure hearts
in a home
are always
within
whispering
distance of
heaven.*

—

Unknown

Stitch Count: 146 x 146

51

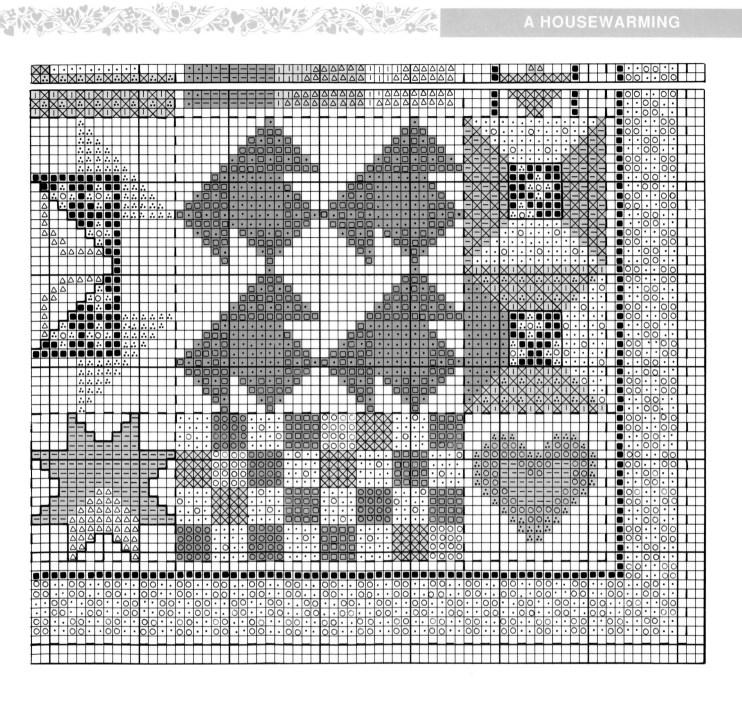

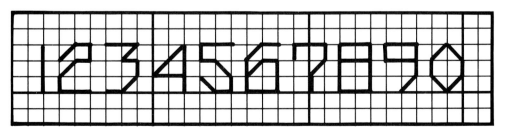

A Housewarming

Stitched on tea-dyed Linen 28 over 2 threads, the finished design size is 10⅜" x 10⅜". The fabric was cut 17" x 17".

FABRICS	DESIGN SIZES
Aida 11	13¼" x 13¼"
Aida 14	10⅜" x 10⅜"
Aida 18	8⅛" x 8⅛"
Hardanger 22	6⅝" x 6⅝"

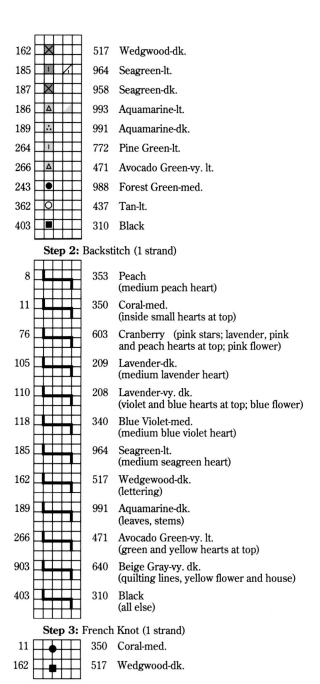

Anchor   **DMC (used for sample)**

Step 1: Cross-stitch (2 strands)

Anchor		DMC	
300		745	Yellow-lt. pale
297		743	Yellow-med.
366		951	Peach Pecan-lt.
8		353	Peach
10		352	Coral-lt.
11		350	Coral-med.
24		776	Pink-med.
26		894	Carnation-vy. lt.
28		892	Carnation-med.
50		605	Cranberry-vy. lt.
75		604	Cranberry-lt.
76		603	Cranberry
108		211	Lavender-lt.
105		209	Lavender-dk.
110		208	Lavender-vy. dk.
117		3747	Blue Violet-vy. lt.
118		340	Blue Violet-med.
119		333	Blue Violet-dk.
158		828	Blue-ultra vy. lt.
130		809	Delft
167		519	Sky Blue
168		518	Wedgwood-lt..
162		517	Wedgwood-dk.
185		964	Seagreen-lt.
187		958	Seagreen-dk.
186		993	Aquamarine-lt.
189		991	Aquamarine-dk.
264		772	Pine Green-lt.
266		471	Avocado Green-vy. lt.
243		988	Forest Green-med.
362		437	Tan-lt.
403		310	Black

Step 2: Backstitch (1 strand)

Anchor		DMC	
8		353	Peach (medium peach heart)
11		350	Coral-med. (inside small hearts at top)
76		603	Cranberry (pink stars; lavender, pink and peach hearts at top; pink flower)
105		209	Lavender-dk. (medium lavender heart)
110		208	Lavender-vy. dk. (violet and blue hearts at top; blue flower)
118		340	Blue Violet-med. (medium blue violet heart)
185		964	Seagreen-lt. (medium seagreen heart)
162		517	Wedgewood-dk. (lettering)
189		991	Aquamarine-dk. (leaves, stems)
266		471	Avocado Green-vy. lt. (green and yellow hearts at top)
903		640	Beige Gray-vy. dk. (quilting lines, yellow flower and house)
403		310	Black (all else)

Step 3: French Knot (1 strand)

Anchor		DMC	
11		350	Coral-med.
162		517	Wedgwood-dk.

Handy Maiden

MATERIALS

Five completed design pieces from pages 57 and 58
   stitched on cream Murano
⅝ yard of unstitched cream Murano;
   matching thread
½ yard of muslin; matching thread
Scraps of six print fabrics; matching threads
1¼ yard of ¼"-wide green jute
⅝ yard of ⅛"-wide elastic
Seventeen assorted buttons
Dark brown wool roving
Two spools of thread
Plastic bobbin
Miniature clothespin
Polyester stuffing
Tracing paper
Dressmaker's pen
Acrylic paints: blue, pink, black, white
Paintbrushes
Hot glue gun and glue sticks
6 to 8 large tea bags

DIRECTIONS
All seam allowances are ¼".

1. Trim house design piece to a 3" square, spools design piece to a 2⅝" square and flower basket design piece to a 2¾" square. Trim three flowers and single pink flower design pieces to 4" x 1½". Make patterns for doll, face and clothes (pages 58–62). Make Templates A, B, C and D (page 63). From muslin, cut two doll body pieces. From unstitched Murano, cut one skirt front and two skirt backs.

2. Cut fifteen each of Templates A, B, C and D from print fabrics and remaining Murano. Join fabric templates as desired, to make a 24" x 24" patchwork square, planning the dress front so it has three flowers and single pink flower design pieces on either shoulder. From patchwork, cut one bodice front on fold, two bodice backs, one hat and two hat brims.

3. Make doll. With right sides facing, stitch doll body pieces, leaving bottom open. Turn. Stuff arms firmly. Stuff head and body firmly. Slipstitch bottom closed. Transfer facial features to doll. Paint eyes blue, pupils black, lips and cheeks pink; outline remaining features in black. Accent pupils with white. Allow to dry. Frame face with dark brown roving arranged in desired hairstyle. Glue in place.

4. Make bodice. With right sides facing, stitch one bodice back to bodice front at shoulder seam and along sleeve top. Repeat. To make casing, fold sleeve ends ¼" double to wrong side of fabric. Stitch close to first folded edge through all layers. From elastic, cut two 4" lengths. Thread elastic through casing. Stitch bodice at side seams and along sleeve bottoms, securing elastic in casings. Trim excess elastic.

5. Make skirt. Machine zigzag edges of house design piece. Topstitch to skirt front, placing as desired. Fray edges of spools design piece. Topstitch to skirt front. Fold edges of flower basket design piece under ¼" to wrong side. Topstitch to skirt front. With right sides facing, stitch skirt backs at center seam beginning 7" from top edge. This opening is to insert pajamas or sewing scraps in the skirt when the doll is completed. Stitch skirt front to back, leaving top open. Sew gathering stitches along top edge of skirt. Match center fronts of bodice and skirt. Gather to fit around bodice bottom. With right sides facing, stitch skirt to bodice bottom.

6. Tea-dye dress. Set washer for small load; fill with hot water. Add six to eight large teabags. Allow dress to agitate until desired shade is achieved; the wet fabric will be slightly darker than when dry. Dry in automatic dryer at appropriate setting; air drying may produce water streaks.

7. Finish dress. Fold neckline ¼" double to wrong side of fabric. Stitch close to first folded edge through all layers. From elastic, cut one 6" length. Thread elastic through casing. Slide dress on doll. Secure ends of elastic in center back. Slipstitch bodice back closed; leave a 6"-long opening in skirt.

8. Make hat. With right sides facing, stitch brims, leaving straight edge open. Turn. Match top center of hat with brim center. With right sides facing, stitch straight edges of brim to hat. Place hat on doll head. Hem raw edge at bottom of hat. Tack A to A on brim, making tuck in hat.

9. Finish doll. Using green floss, finish edges of house design piece with large, loose cross-stitches. Using brown floss, buttonhole-stitch edges of flower basket design piece with blanket stitches. Sew eight buttons to skirt as desired. To make necklace, cut one 9" length of jute, separating one strand; thread with nine buttons, working buttons to center of jute. Discard remaining separated strand. Tie necklace around doll neck. Clip miniature clothespin to necklace center. To make belt, tie remaining 36" length of jute around doll waist, leaving matching tails hanging free. String spools and bobbin to jute tails at varying lengths. Secure with knots.

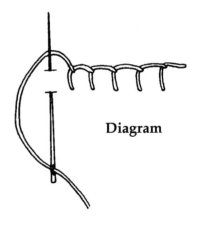

Diagram

Stitch Count: 30 x 30

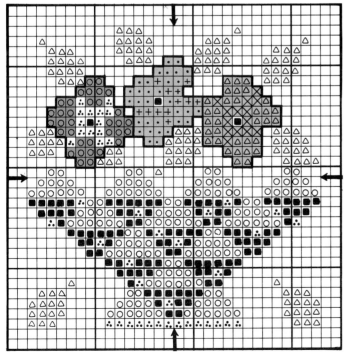

Stitch Count: 32 x 32

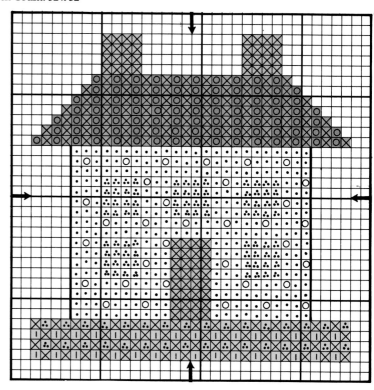

Stitch Count: 32 x 32

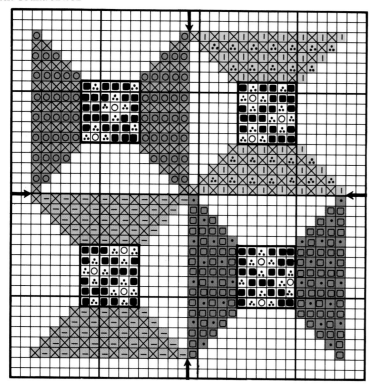

Handy Maiden Face

58

Flower basket: Stitched on cream Murano 30 over 2 threads, the finished design size is 2" x 2". The fabric was cut 6" x 6".

Three flowers: The flowers motif was taken from the flower basket motif. Stitched on cream Murano 30 over 2 threads, the finished design size is 1⅞" x ⅞". The fabric was cut 4" x 1½".

Single pink flower: The flower motif was taken from the flower basket motif. Stitched on cream Murano 30 over 2 threads, the finished design size is ¾" x ⅞". The fabric was cut 4" x 1½".

House and spools: Stitched on cream Murano 30 over 2 threads, the finished design sizes are 2⅛" x 2⅛". The fabric was cut 6" x 6" for each.

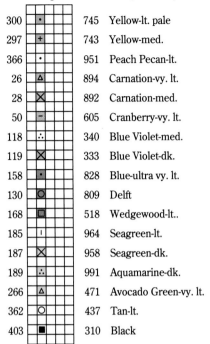

Anchor		DMC (used for sample)	
Step 1: Cross-stitch (2 strands)			
300	•	745	Yellow-lt. pale
297	+	743	Yellow-med.
366	•	951	Peach Pecan-lt.
26	△	894	Carnation-vy. lt.
28	✕	892	Carnation-med.
50	▬	605	Cranberry-vy. lt.
118	∴	340	Blue Violet-med.
119	✕	333	Blue Violet-dk.
158	▪	828	Blue-ultra vy. lt.
130	○	809	Delft
168	▢	518	Wedgewood-lt..
185	ı	964	Seagreen-lt.
187	✕	958	Seagreen-dk.
189	∴	991	Aquamarine-dk.
266	△	471	Avocado Green-vy. lt.
362	○	437	Tan-lt.
403	■	310	Black
Step 2: Backstitch (1 strand)			
76		603	Cranberry (pink flower)
110		208	Lavender-vy. dk. (blue flower)
903		640	Beige Gray-vy. dk. (yellow flower, house)
403		310	Black (all else)

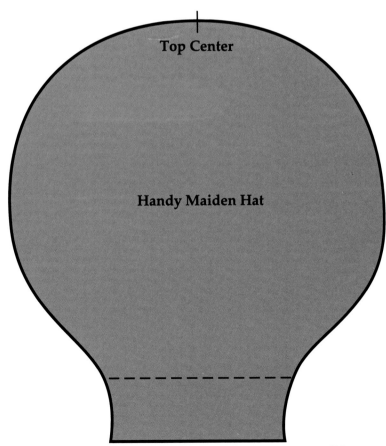

Top Center

Handy Maiden Hat

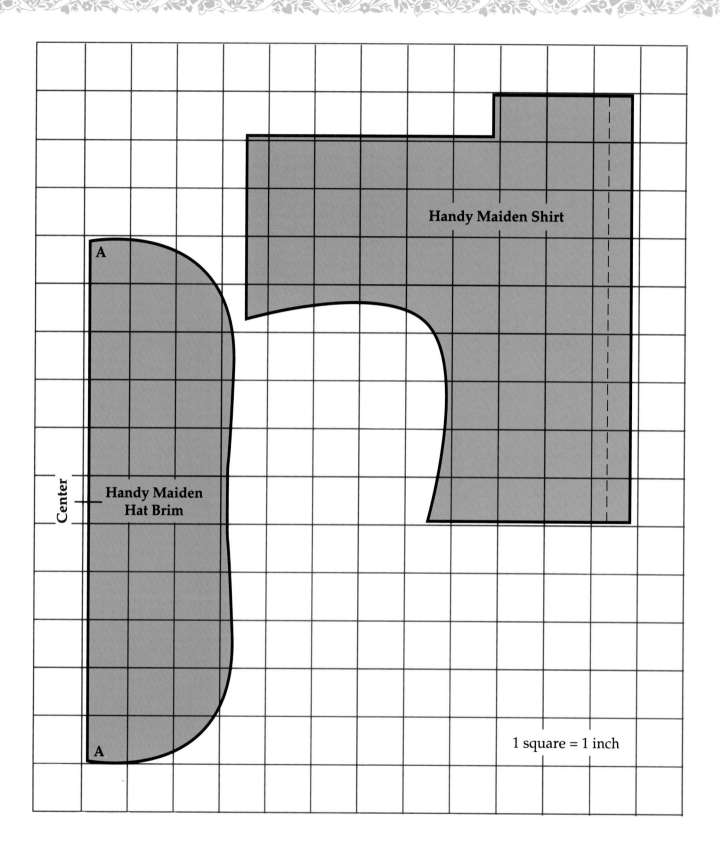

Handy Maiden Shirt

A

Center

Handy Maiden
Hat Brim

A

1 square = 1 inch

60

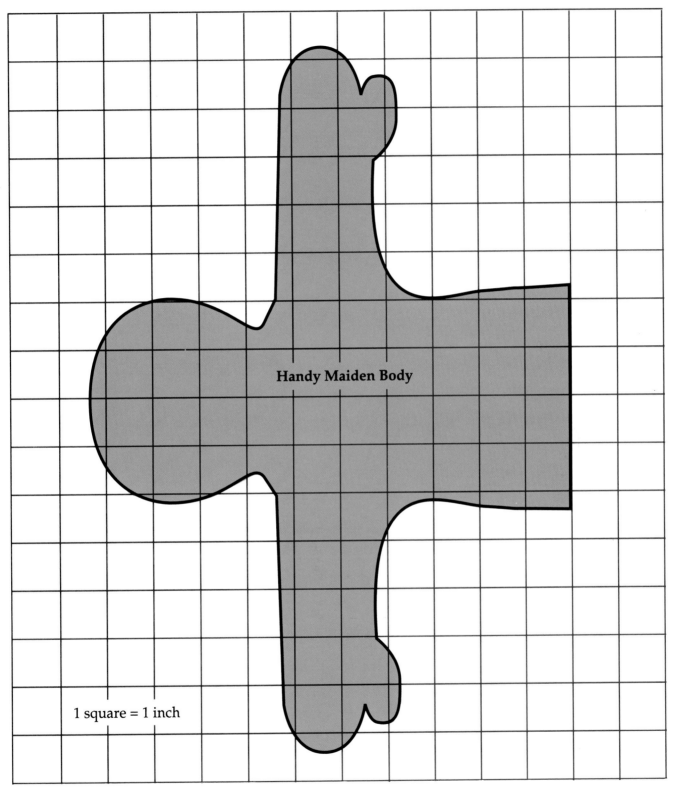

Handy Maiden Body

1 square = 1 inch

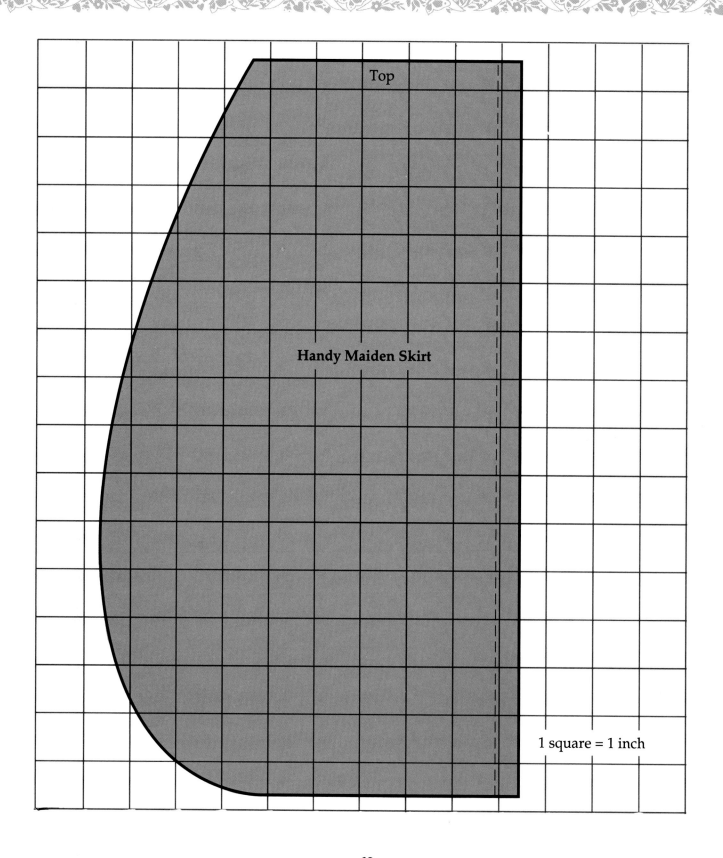

Top

Handy Maiden Skirt

1 square = 1 inch

62

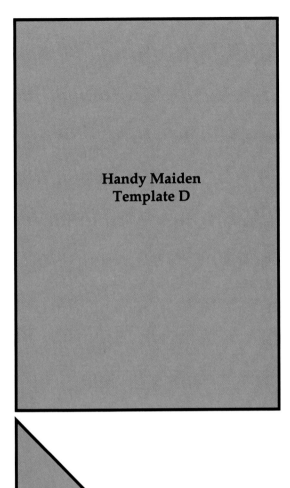

Handy Maiden
Template D

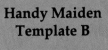

Handy Maiden
Template B

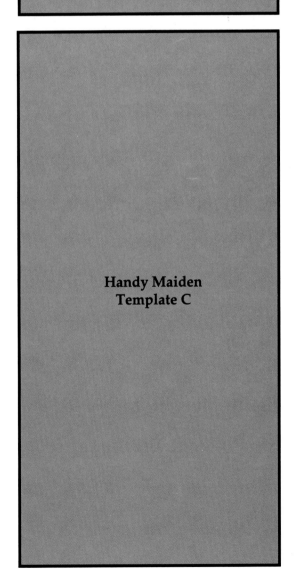

Handy Maiden
Template C

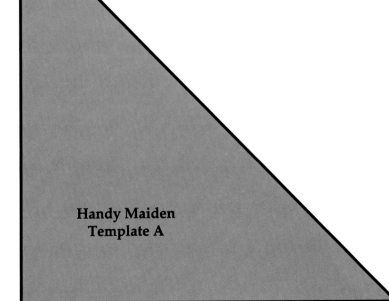

Handy Maiden
Template A

*Friendship
cannot be
bought, begged,
borrowed or
stolen, for it is
something that
is of no earthly
good to
someone until
it is given
away.*

—

Unknown

Welcome Friends

Stitched on white Linen 28 over 2 threads, the finished design size is 6¼" x 10⅜". The fabric was cut 13" x 17".

FABRICS	DESIGN SIZES
Aida 11	8" x 13¼"
Aida 14	6¼" x 10⅜"
Aida 18	4⅞" x 8⅛"
Hardanger 22	4" x 6⅝"

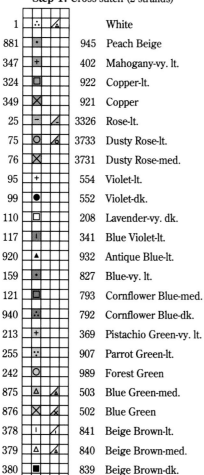

Anchor		DMC (used for sample)	
Step 1: Cross-stitch (2 strands)			
1			White
881		945	Peach Beige
347		402	Mahogany-vy. lt.
324		922	Copper-lt.
349		921	Copper
25		3326	Rose-lt.
75		3733	Dusty Rose-lt.
76		3731	Dusty Rose-med.
95		554	Violet-lt.
99		552	Violet-dk.
110		208	Lavender-vy. dk.
117		341	Blue Violet-lt.
920		932	Antique Blue-lt.
159		827	Blue-vy. lt.
121		793	Cornflower Blue-med.
940		792	Cornflower Blue-dk.
213		369	Pistachio Green-vy. lt.
255		907	Parrot Green-lt.
242		989	Forest Green
875		503	Blue Green-med.
876		502	Blue Green
378		841	Beige Brown-lt.
379		840	Beige Brown-med.
380		839	Beige Brown-dk.

Continued on page 68.

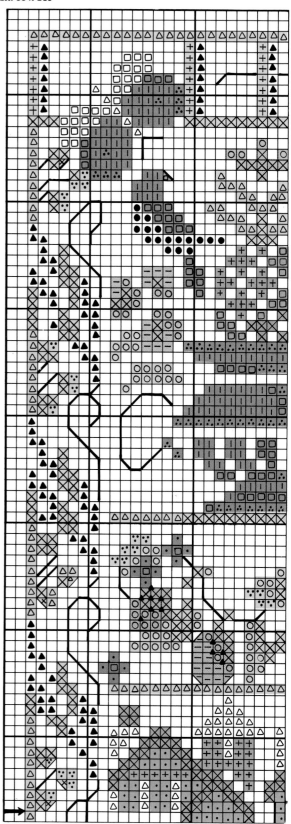

Continued from page 66.

Step 2: Backstitch (1 strand)

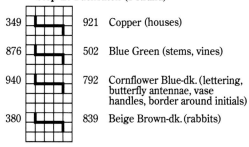

349		921	Copper (houses)
876		502	Blue Green (stems, vines)
940		792	Cornflower Blue-dk. (lettering, butterfly antennae, vase handles, border around initials)
380		839	Beige Brown-dk. (rabbits)

Step 3: French Knot (1 strand)

| 940 | ● | 792 | Cornflower Blue-dk. |
| 380 | ▲ | 839 | Beige Brown-dk. |

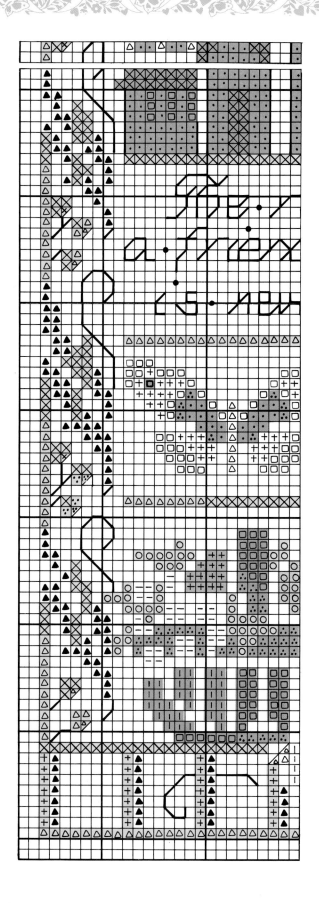

Painted Posies

Butterfly border:
Stitched on white Dublin Linen 25 over 2 threads, the design is taken from the sampler on pages 68 and 69; it is located under the houses. Stitch five repeats. The fabric was cut 19" x 4"; cut two lengths.

MATERIALS

Completed design piece on white Dublin Linen
Purchased 8½"-tall metal pitcher
Metal primer spray
Acrylic paints: off-white, purple, lavender, light
 blue, dark blue, light green, dark green,
 blue-green, orange, peach, brown, rose, pink,
 gray-blue
Stencilling brushes
Craft knife
10" x 10" sheet of frosted Mylar
10" x 10" piece of mat board
Drafting tape
Tracing paper
Soft lead pencil

DIRECTIONS

1. Make vase stencil pattern (page 72). Transfer to Mylar with soft lead pencil. Tape Mylar to mat board. Using craft knife, cut out areas to be stencilled. Cut stencil apart.

2. Spray pitcher with primer. Allow to dry. Using paintbrush, paint pitcher interior and exterior with three coats of off-white paint, allowing paint to dry thoroughly between coats. Tape stencil to front center of pitcher. Stencil, using desired colors. Allow to dry.

3. Fold long edges of one stitched border piece under 1¼". Place border piece ½" below pitcher rim. Fold one short edge under and overlap at back of pitcher. Slipstitch edges together tightly. Repeat, placing remaining border piece ½" from bottom edge.

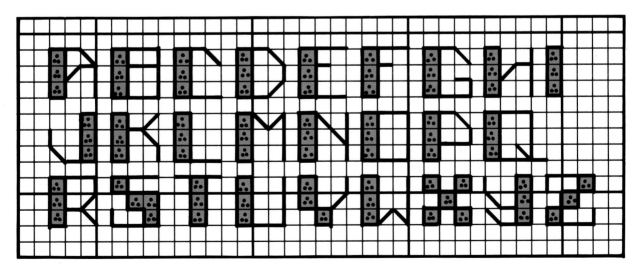

Alphabet for personalizing initials in sampler on pages 66–69.

Vase Stencil

Stitch Count: 72 x 46

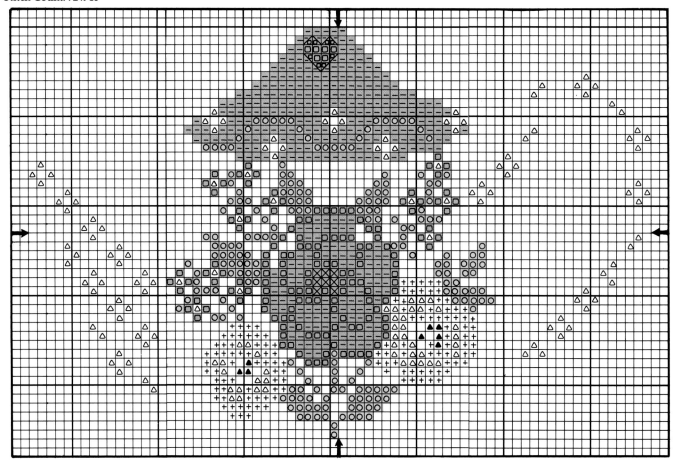

Friendship's Brewing

Pink rose teapot:

Stitched on white Jobelan 28 over 2 threads, the finished design size is 5⅛" x 3¼". The fabric was cut 10" x 8".

Anchor		DMC (used for sample)	
		Step 1: Cross-stitch (2 strands)	
48	− ◿	818	Baby Pink
25	▢ ◿	3326	Rose-lt.
76	✕	3731	Dusty Rose-med.
95	+	554	Violet-lt.
110	△	208	Lavender-vy. dk.
101	▲	550	Violet-vy. dk.
242	○	989	Forest Green

MATERIALS (for one)

Completed design on white Jobelan 28
One 7" x 10" piece of mat board
Craft knife
Tracing paper
7" x 5" piece of fleece
7" x 5" piece of coordinating print fabric
1 yard of coordinating small rayon cord
Dressmaker's pen
Spray adhesive

DIRECTIONS

1. Make teapot pattern (page 140). To make teapot cutouts, trace pattern onto mat board twice. Cut out with craft knife. Trace teapot pattern onto right side of design piece with dressmaker's pen. Cut out design piece for front ½" outside of outline.

Trace teapot pattern onto print fabric. Cut out back ½" outside of outline. From fleece, cut one front like pattern.

2. Using spray adhesive, attach fleece to right side of teapot front cutout. Center cutout/fleece over wrong side of design piece, placing fleece against wrong side of design. Clip edges of fabric. Pulling snugly, wrap and glue edges to wrong side. Repeat to make back, wrapping print fabric around cutout. Glue teapot front to back.

3. Cut one 5" and one 10" piece of cord. Make a loop and knot 10" piece near end. Glue ends to center top on back of design piece for hanger. Glue 5" cord piece along inside edge of handle. Glue remaining cord along outside edge of teapot, beginning in sharp corner near handle.

House motif teapot:
Stitched on white Jobelan 28 over 2 threads, the finished design size is 5⅜" x 3¼". The fabric was cut 10" x 8".

Anchor		DMC (used for sample)	
Step 1: Cross-stitch (2 strands)			
76	I	3731	Dusty Rose-med.
159	▵	827	Blue-vy. lt.
940	◉	792	Cornflower Blue-dk.
242	○	989	Forest Green
876	·	502	Blue Green
347	−	402	Mahogany-vy. lt.
349	X	921	Copper
Step 2: Backstitch (1 strand)			
940		792	Cornflower Blue-dk.

Stitch Count: 75 x 45

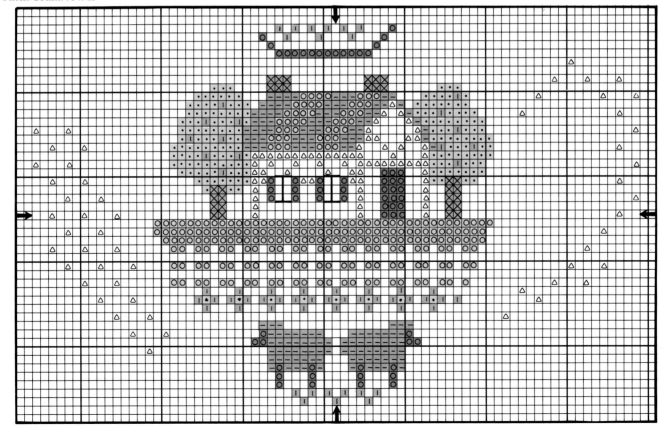

Stitch count: 73 x 53

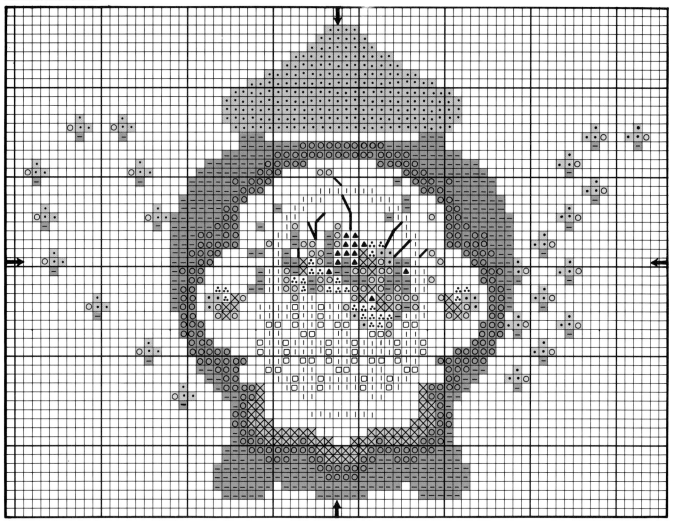

Floral basket teapot:

Stitched on white Jobelan 28 over 2 threads, the finished design size is 5¼" x 3¾". The fabric was cut 10" x 8".

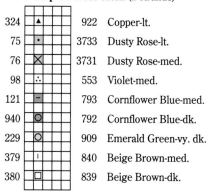

Anchor		DMC (used for sample)	
		Step 1: Cross-stitch (2 strands)	
324	▲	922	Copper-lt.
75	•	3733	Dusty Rose-lt.
76	✕	3731	Dusty Rose-med.
98	∴	553	Violet-med.
121	−	793	Cornflower Blue-med.
940	⊙	792	Cornflower Blue-dk.
229	○	909	Emerald Green-vy. dk.
379	I	840	Beige Brown-med.
380	☐	839	Beige Brown-dk.

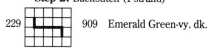

		Step 2: Backstitch (1 strand)	
229		909	Emerald Green-vy. dk.

Stitch count: 70 x 49

Blue flowers teapot:
Stitched on white Jobelan 28 over 2 threads, the
finished design size is 5" x 3½". The fabric was cut
9" x 8".

Anchor		DMC (used for sample)	
		Step 1: Cross-stitch (2 strands)	
881	I	945	Peach Beige
349	□	921	Copper
159	·	827	Blue-vy. lt.
121	✕	793	Cornflower Blue-med.
242	○	989	Forest Green
		Step 2: Backstitch (1 strand)	
349		921	Copper
		Step 3: French Knot (1 strand)	
121	●	793	Cornflower Blue-med.

*Every child
comes with the
message that
God is not yet
discouraged of
man.*

—

Rabindranath Tagore

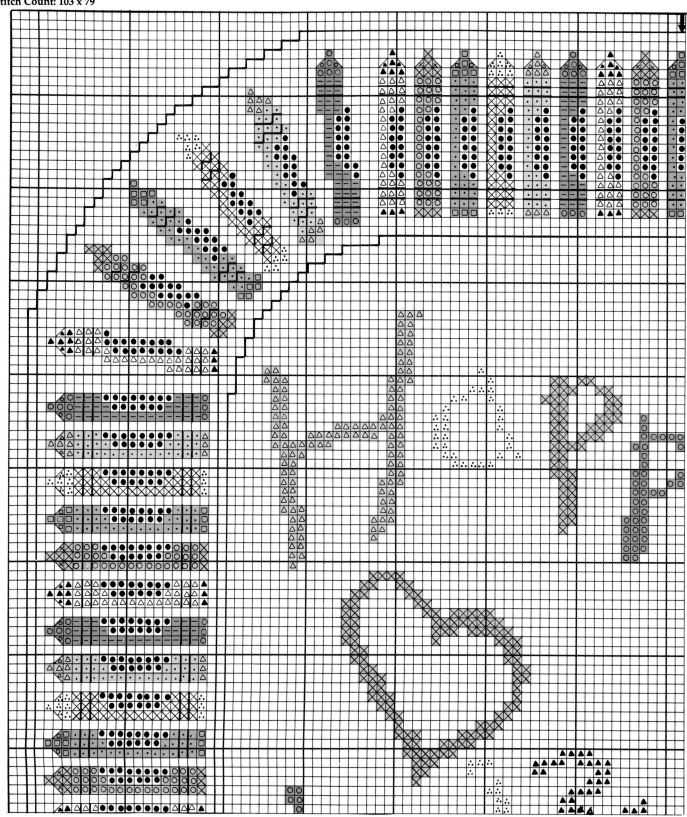

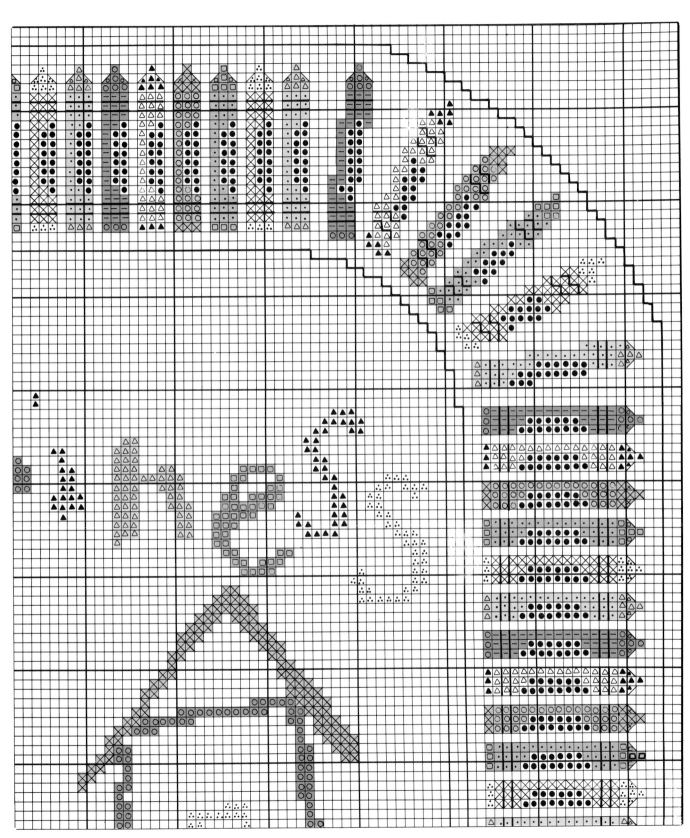

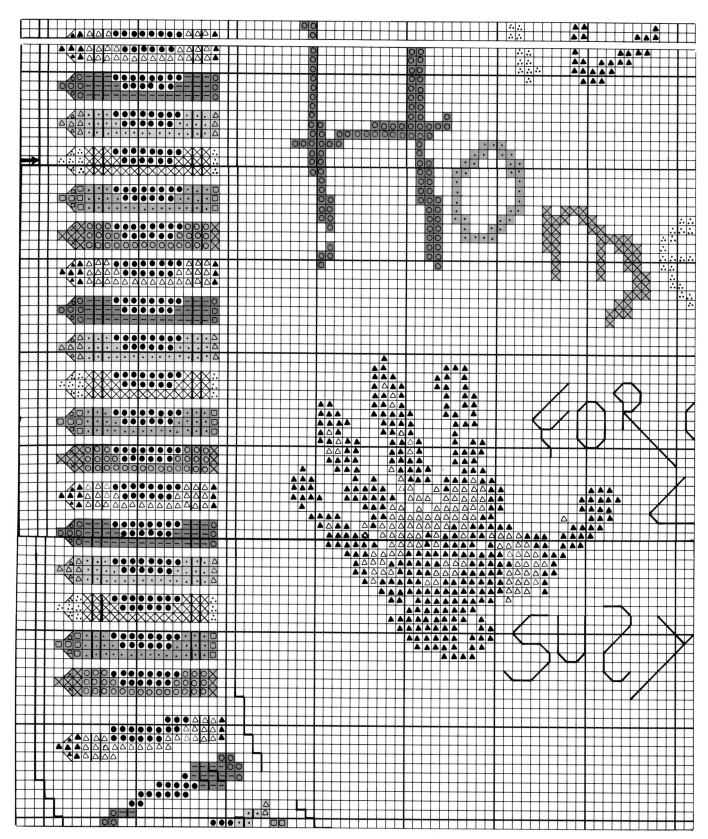

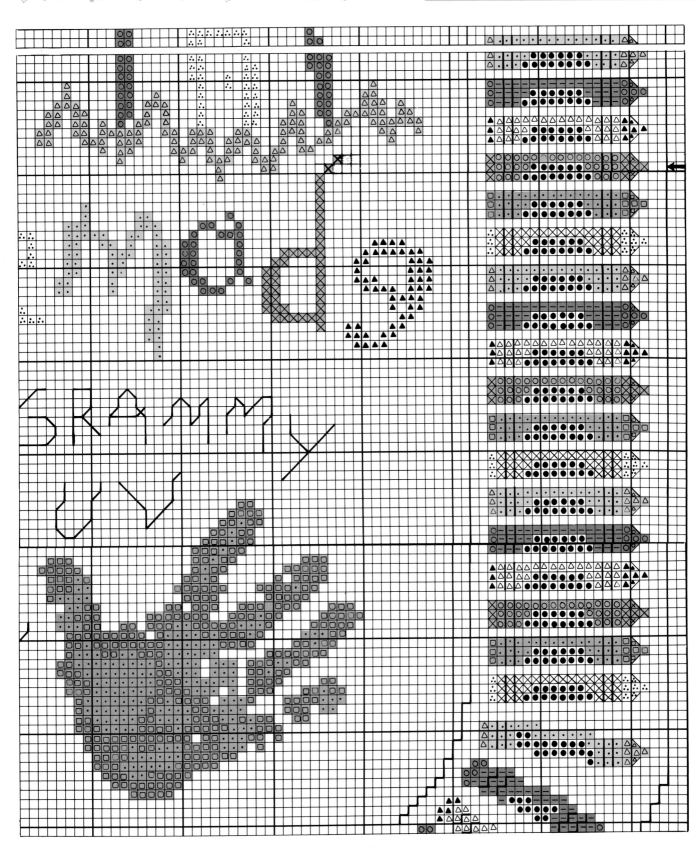

Stitch Count: 145 x 193

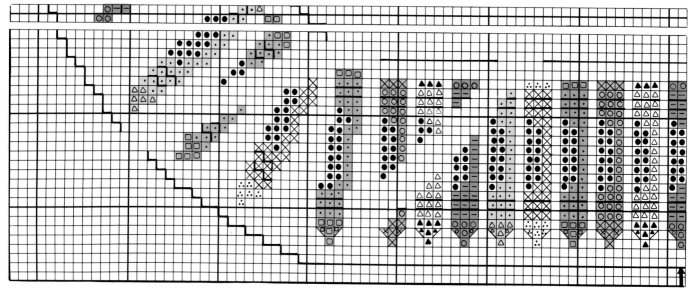

The Color of Love

Stitched on white Aida 14 over 1 thread, the finished design size is 10⅜" x 13¾". The fabric was cut 17" x 20".

FABRICS	DESIGN SIZES
Aida 11	13⅛" x 17½"
Aida 18	8⅛" x 10¾"
Hardanger 22	6⅝" x 8¾"

Anchor			DMC (used for sample)	
			Step 1: Cross-stitch (2 strands)	
293	X		727	Topaz-vy. lt.
297	∴	◢	743	Yellow-med.
304	•		741	Tangerine-med.
333	□	◢	608	Orange Red
35	○		3705	Melon-dk.
46	X	◢	666	Christmas Red-bright
95	△		554	Violet-lt.
110	▲	◢	208	Lavender-vy. dk.
130	–		809	Delft
132	○	◢	797	Royal Blue
256	•		704	Chartreuse-bright
227	△	◢	701	Christmas Green-lt.
403	●		310	Black

			Step 2: Backstitch (1 strand)	
403			310	Black

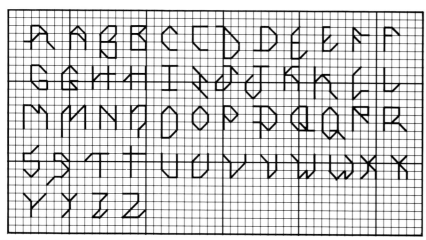

Alphabet for personalizing towel on page 89.

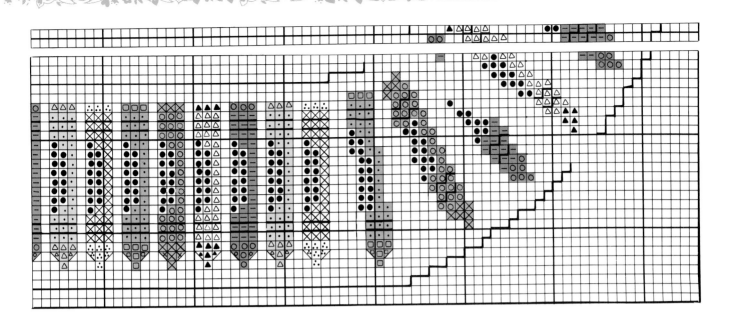

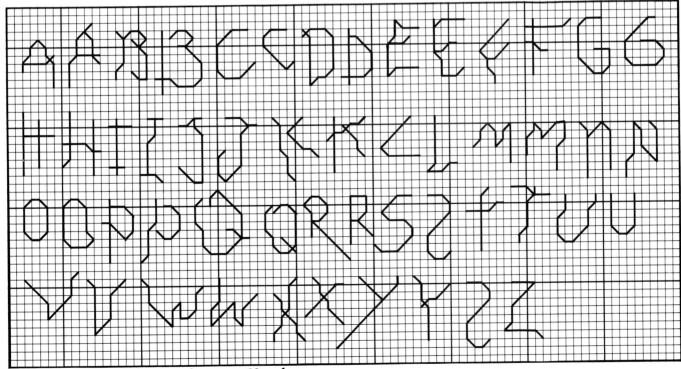

Alphabet for personalizing towel on page 89 and sampler on pages 80-85

85

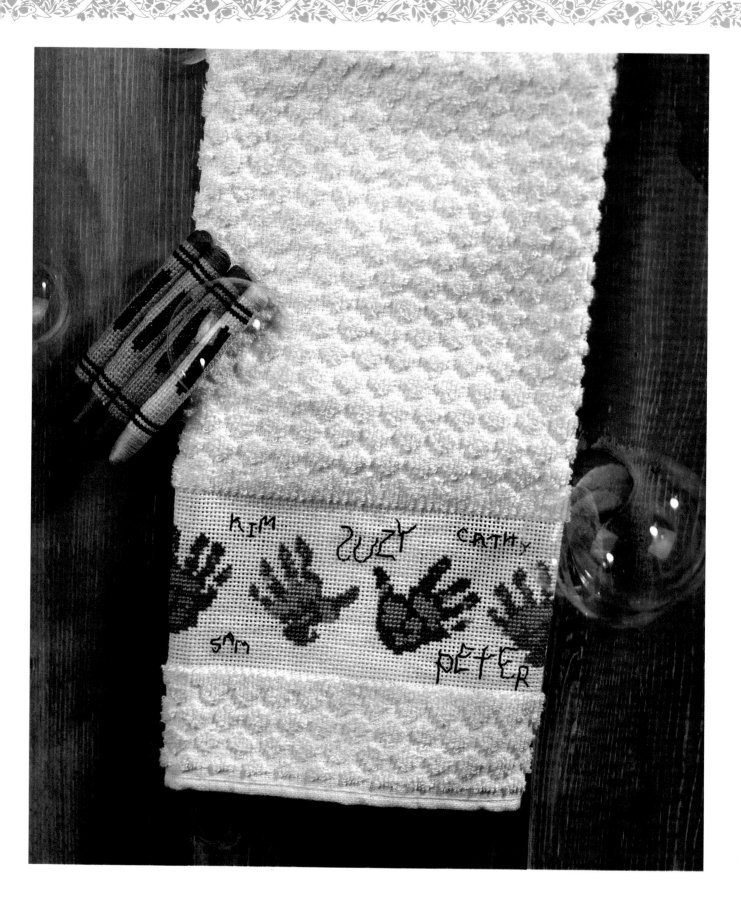

Rainbow Barrette

Stitched on white Aida 14 over 1 thread, the finished design size for one crayon is 1⅛" x 3⅝". The fabric was cut 6" x 6". Stitch four crayons.

FABRICS	DESIGN SIZES
Aida 11	1⅜" x 4½"
Aida 18	⅞" x 2¾"
Hardanger 22	⅝" x 2¼"

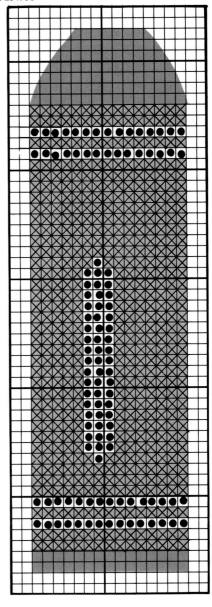

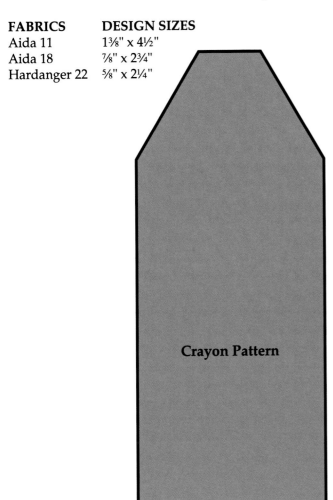

Crayon Pattern

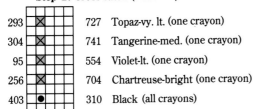

Anchor		DMC (used for sample)

Step 1: Cross-stitch (2 strands)

293	☒	727	Topaz-vy. lt. (one crayon)
304	☒	741	Tangerine-med. (one crayon)
95	☒	554	Violet-lt. (one crayon)
256	☒	704	Chartreuse-bright (one crayon)
403	●	310	Black (all crayons)

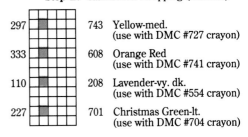

Step 2: Satin Stitch Wrapping (1 strand)

297		743	Yellow-med. (use with DMC #727 crayon)
333		608	Orange Red (use with DMC #741 crayon)
110		208	Lavender-vy. dk. (use with DMC #554 crayon)
227		701	Christmas Green-lt. (use with DMC #704 crayon)

Stitch Count: 161 x 38

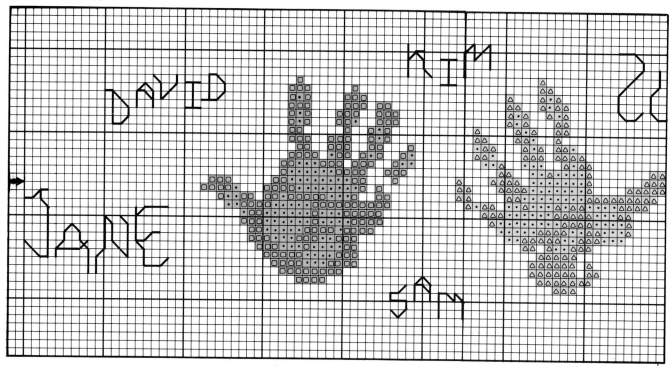

MATERIALS

Purchased 3"-wide clasp barrette
Completed design pieces on white Aida 14;
    matching thread
Embroidery floss: to match stitching
Polyester stuffing
Tracing paper
Dressmaker's pen
Liquid ravel preventer
Hot glue gun and glue sticks

DIRECTIONS
All seams are ¼".

1. Make pattern for crayon. With design centered, cut one crayon from each completed design piece. Apply ravel preventer to fabric edges. Allow to dry overnight.

2. With right sides facing, fold one crayon in half so that long edges meet. Stitch around crayon tip and ½" of long edges. Turn. Press long edges ¼" to

wrong side of fabric. Press bottom edge under ½". Stuff tip. Whipstitch long edges. Stuff firmly. Repeat with remaining crayons.

3. Using satin stitch, cover tip of one crayon with matching floss (see diagram). Wind floss around satin stitching (see diagram). Apply ravel preventer to tip to hold stitching in place. Repeat with crayon end. Repeat with remaining crayons.

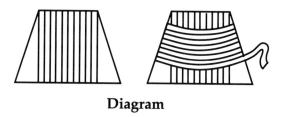

Diagram

4. Lay crayons side-by-side with tips and ends aligned and stitched areas facing up. Glue long edges of crayons together. Allow glue to dry. Whipstitch barrette to back center of crayons.

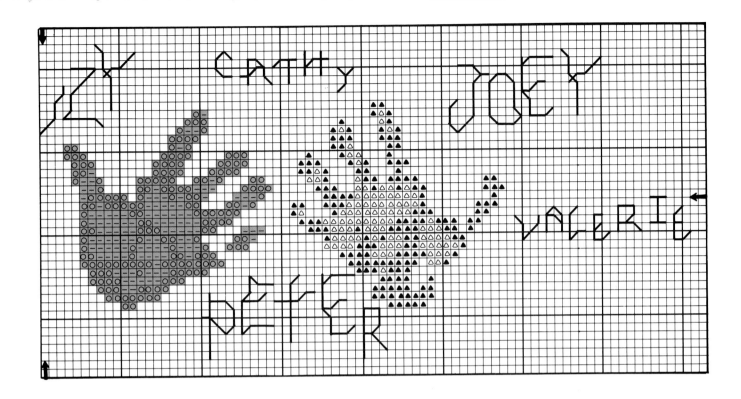

From a Cherished Child

Stitched on white Estate Towel 14 over 1 thread, the finished design size is 11½" x 2¾". To personalize your towel, replace these letters with the letters in the alphabet on page 85.

FABRICS | **DESIGN SIZES**
Aida 11 | 14⅝" x 3½"
Aida 18 | 9" x 2⅛"
Hardanger 22 | 7⅜" x 1¾"

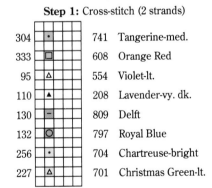

Anchor		DMC (used for sample)	
		Step 1: Cross-stitch (2 strands)	
304	•	741	Tangerine-med.
333	□	608	Orange Red
95	△	554	Violet-lt.
110	▲	208	Lavender-vy. dk.
130	−	809	Delft
132	○	797	Royal Blue
256	•	704	Chartreuse-bright
227	△	701	Christmas Green-lt.
		Step 2: Backstitch (1 strand)	
403		310	Black

Welcome Reflections

Stitched on white Aida 14 over 1 thread, the finished design size is 7⅜" x 5⅝". The fabric was cut 14" x 12". We recommend taking design piece and mirror to a professional framer.

FABRICS	DESIGN SIZES
Aida 11	9⅜" x 7⅛"
Aida 18	5¾" x 4¾"
Hardanger 22	4⅝" x 3⅝"

Anchor		DMC (used for sample)	
Step 1: Cross-stitch (2 strands)			
293	X	727	Topaz-vy. lt.
304	·	741	Tangerine-med.
347	–	402	Mahogany-vy. lt.
324	··	922	Copper-lt.
46	X	666	Christmas Red-bright
87	☐	3607	Plum-lt.
130		809	Delft
132	○	797	Royal Blue
256	·	704	Chartreuse-bright
227	△	701	Christmas Green-lt.
403	●	310	Black

Anchor		DMC (used for sample)	
Step 2: Backstitch (1 strand)			
355		975	Golden Brown-dk. (bear)
403		310	Black (all else)

MATERIALS

Completed design piece on white Aida 14
14" x 20" piece of green mat board
14" x 10" piece of red mat board
6" x 10" mirror
14½" x 20" wooden frame 1¾" wide
3½" x 12" piece of green mat board in a ¾"-wide frame for shelf

Remind Me to Smile

Stitched on white Aida 14 over 1 thread, the finished design is 12¾" x 4¼". The fabric was cut 19" x 11". We recommend taking the design piece and cork board to a professional framer.

FABRICS   **DESIGN SIZES**
Aida 11   16⅛" x 5½"
Aida 18   9⅞" x 3⅜"
Hardanger 22 8" x 2¾"

MATERIALS

Completed design piece on white Aida 14
20" x 22" piece of red mat board
20" x 22" piece of yellow mat board
10" x 14" cork board
20" x 22" wooden frame ¾" wide

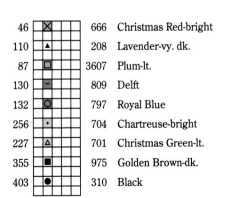

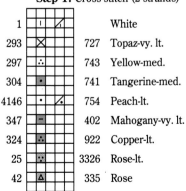

Anchor   DMC (used for sample)

Step 1: Cross-stitch (2 strands)

1			White	
293		727	Topaz-vy. lt.	
297		743	Yellow-med.	
304		741	Tangerine-med.	
4146		754	Peach-lt.	
347		402	Mahogany-vy. lt.	
324		922	Copper-lt.	
25		3326	Rose-lt.	
42		335	Rose	

46		666	Christmas Red-bright	
110		208	Lavender-vy. dk.	
87		3607	Plum-lt.	
130		809	Delft	
132		797	Royal Blue	
256		704	Chartreuse-bright	
227		701	Christmas Green-lt.	
355		975	Golden Brown-dk.	
403		310	Black	

Step 2: Backstitch (1 strand)

46		666	Christmas Red-bright (SPOT, harness)	
132		797	Royal Blue (lettering, numbers)	
355		975	Golden Brown-dk. (flesh, faces, horse, hair)	
403		310	Black (all else)	

*No cord or
cable can draw
so forcibly, or
bind so fast, as
love can do
with a single
thread.*

—

Robert Burton

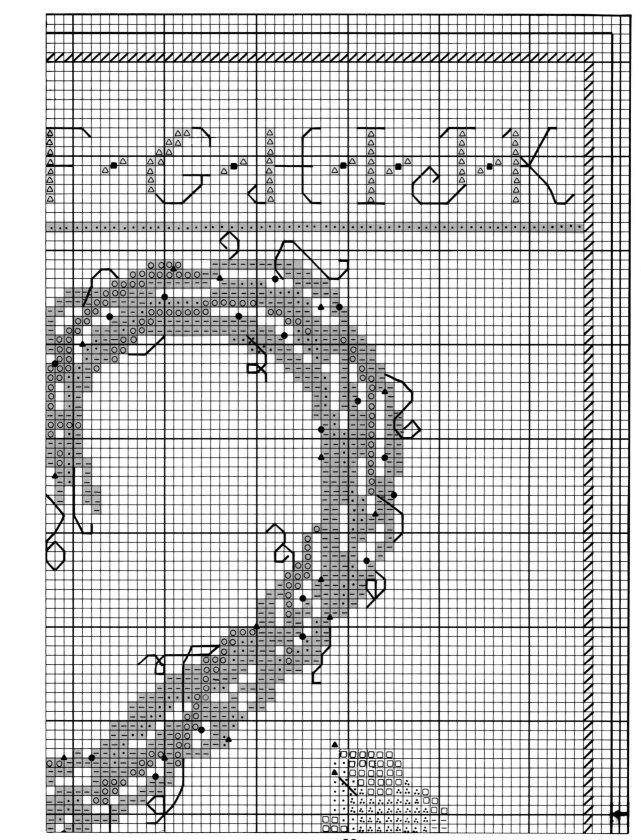

A Gift from the Heart

Stitched on amber Linen 28 over 2 threads, the finished design size is 8⅞" x 11⅞". The fabric was cut 15" x 18".

FABRICS	DESIGN SIZES
Aida 11	11⅜" x 15⅛"
Aida 14	8⅞" x 11⅞"
Aida 18	7" x 9¼"
Hardanger 22	5⅝" x 7½"

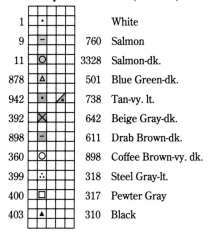

Anchor		DMC (used for sample)
Step 1: Cross-stitch (2 strands)		
1	·	White
9	–	760 Salmon
11	○	3328 Salmon-dk.
878	△	501 Blue Green-dk.
942	· ╱	738 Tan-vy. lt.
392	⊠	642 Beige Gray-dk.
898	–	611 Drab Brown-dk.
360	◎	898 Coffee Brown-vy. dk.
399	∴	318 Steel Gray-lt.
400	□	317 Pewter Gray
403	▲	310 Black

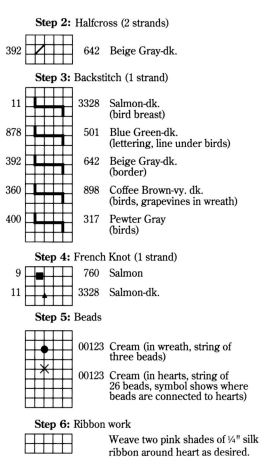

Step 2: Halfcross (2 strands)

392 ╱ 642 Beige Gray-dk.

Step 3: Backstitch (1 strand)

11   3328 Salmon-dk. (bird breast)

878   501 Blue Green-dk. (lettering, line under birds)

392   642 Beige Gray-dk. (border)

360   898 Coffee Brown-vy. dk. (birds, grapevines in wreath)

400   317 Pewter Gray (birds)

Step 4: French Knot (1 strand)

9 ■ 760 Salmon

11 ▲ 3328 Salmon-dk.

Step 5: Beads

●   00123 Cream (in wreath, string of three beads)

✕   00123 Cream (in hearts, string of 26 beads, symbol shows where beads are connected to hearts)

Step 6: Ribbon work

Weave two pink shades of ¼" silk ribbon around heart as desired.

Love Birds

Stitched on white Gloria Cloth 14 over 1 thread, the finished design size is 7⅞" x 6¾". The fabric was cut 52½" x 53½". Instead of a crocheted edging, upholstery or drapery trim can be used to finish the afghan edges.

FABRICS	DESIGN SIZES
Aida 11	10" x 8⅝"
Aida 18	6⅛" x 5¼"
Hardanger 22	5" x 4⅜"

MATERIALS

Completed design on white Gloria Cloth 14
Yarn description: Bedspread-weight crochet cotton (50 gr., 218 yd. ball) three balls medium pink.
Yarn pictured: DMC Brilliant Knitting/Crochet Cotton (50 gr., 218 yd. ball) three balls #3326.
Tools and equipment: Size 5 steel crochet hook or size to obtain gauge
Gauge: 10 Shells = 7"

DIRECTIONS

Fabric preparation: Trim all edges even. With sewing machine or serger, zigzag around all four edges of the afghan. Turn finished edge under ¼" to the wrong side and crochet over it.

Rnd 1: Join thread with sc in corner of afghan; beginning at long side, ch 1, sc in same corner, working in spaces between the fabric threads: * sc across having 1 sc every other sp (our model has 378 sts), (sc, ch 1, sc) in corner sp, work sc across short side of afghan in same manner (our model has 366 sts), **(sc, ch 1, sc) in corner sp, rep from * once ending at * *, sl st in beg sc.

Rnd 2: Sl st into corner ch-1 sp, ch 4 for sc and ch 3, 3 dc in same corner, (sk next 4 sts, sc in next st, ch 3, 3 dc in same st for shell) across long side to corner sp, it may be necessary to adjust the number of skipped sts before the corner sp, there will be 75 shells on long sides and 73 shells on short sides plus a shell in each corner space, *sc in corner sp, ch 3, 3 dc in same corner, (sk 4 sts, sc in next st, ch 3, 3 dc in same st) across to next corner sp, rep from * around, end with sl st in base st of beg ch-4.

Crochet Abbreviations:			
beg	begin (ning)	pat(s)	pattern(s)
ch	chain	prev	previous
ch-	chain previously made	rep	repeat
cl	cluster	rnd(s)	round(s)
cont	continu(e) (ing)	sc	single crochet
dc	double crochet	sk	skip
dtr	double triple crochet	sl st	slip stitch
ea	each	sp(s)	space(s)
est	establish(ed)	st(s)	stitch(es)
lp(s)	loop(s)	tr	triple crochet
		yo	yarn over

Rnd 3: Sl st in ea of next 3 ch, sc in same sp as third sl st, (ch 7, sc in next ch-3 sp) around, end with ch 4, dtr in first sc.

Rnd 4: Sc in same 1p just completed, (ch 7, sc in next 1p) around, end with ch 4, dtr in first sc. Note: To work cl: retaining last 1p of ea st on hook: work sts as specified in pat, yo and through all 1ps on hook.

Rnd 5: * Ch 7 (3-tr cl, ch 3, 3-tr cl, ch 3, 3-tr cl) in next 1p for corner, (ch 7, sc in next 1p) 4 times, [ch 7, 3-tr cl in ea of next 3 1ps, (ch 7, sc in next 1p) 5 times] 8 times, ch 7, 3-tr cl in ea of next 3 1ps, (ch 7, sc in next 1p) 3 times, rep between * around, adjust as necessary (all 4 sides should have 9 pat plus corner sections), end with ch 4, tr in base of beg ch-7 to complete last lp.

Rnd 6: Sc in same 1p just completed, ch 7, sc in next 1p, [ch 7, 3-tr cl in next ch-3 sp, between corner clusters, ch 3, 3-tr cl in next ch-3 sp, between clusters, (ch 7, sc in next, 1p) 5 times, * ch 4, tr in sc just made, sc in top of next cl, ch 3, sk next cl, sc in top of next cl, ch 4, tr in sc just made, sc in next 1p,

(ch 7, sc in next 1p) 5 times, rep from * 8 times more,] end last rep with (ch 7, sc in next 1p) 4 times, cont around afghan, rep between [ ], except end with ch 4, tr in first sc to complete last lp.

Rnd 7: Sc in same 1p just completed, (ch 7, sc in next 1p) 8 times, * ch 7, (3-tr cl, ch 5) twice in ch-3 sp, 3-tr cl in same sp, (ch 7, sc in next 1p) 5 times, rep from * 8 times more, end last rep with (ch 7, sc in next 1p) 10 times around corner section, cont around afghan as est and working pat rep as needed, end with ch 4, tr in first sc.

Rnd 8: Sc in same 1p just completed, (ch 7, sc in next 1p) around, ch 4, tr in first sc.

Rnd 9: Sc in same 1p just completed, (ch 7, sc in next 1p) 4 times, * ch 7, (sc, ch 7, sc) in next 1p for corner, (ch 7, sc in next 1p) across to corner 1p, rep from * around, ch 4, tr in first sc.

Rnd 10: Ch 4 for first tr, 2-tr cl in same 1p, * ch 1, (3-tr cl, ch 7, sl st in 4th ch from hook for picot, ch 3, 3-tr cl) in next 1p, rep from * around, end with (3-tr cl, ch 7, picot, ch 3) in beg 1p, sl st in top of beg cl. Fasten off.

Stitch Count: 110 x 95

Anchor		DMC	(used for sample)

Step 1: Cross-stitch (6 strands)

1	·		White
8	□	353	Peach
9	■	760	Salmon
49	·	963	Wild Rose-vy. lt.
25	–	3326	Rose-lt.
27	○ ◢	899	Rose-med.
158	+	775	Baby Blue-vy. lt.
159	△	3325	Baby Blue-lt.
145	⊠	334	Baby Blue-med.
213	ı	369	Pistachio Green-vy. lt.
214	○	368	Pistachio Green-lt.
216	⊠	367	Pistachio Green-dk.
879	∴	890	Pistachio Green-ultra dk.
942	·	738	Tan-vy. lt.
362	□	437	Tan-lt.
309	⊠	435	Brown-vy. lt.
371	∴	433	Brown-med.
399	⊠ ◿	318	Steel Gray-lt.
403	○	310	Black

Step 2: Backstitch (2 strands)

| 403 | | 310 | Black (eyes) |
| 401 | | 535 | Ash Gray-vy. lt. (all else) |

Step 3: Short stitch (2 strands)

| 1 | | | White (highlights in bird's eyes) |

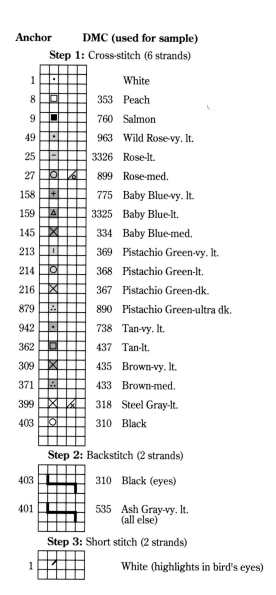

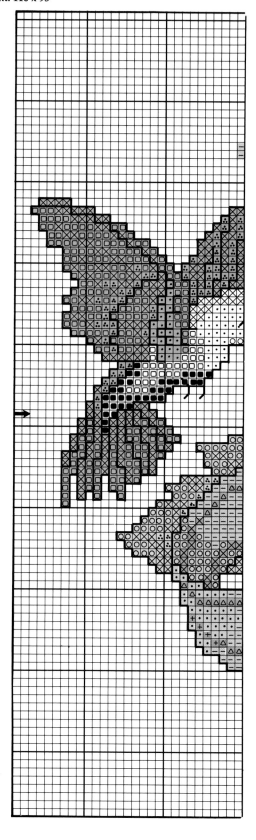

106

A smile is
an invitation
to draw up a
chair before
the log fire of
friendship.

—

Unknown

111

113

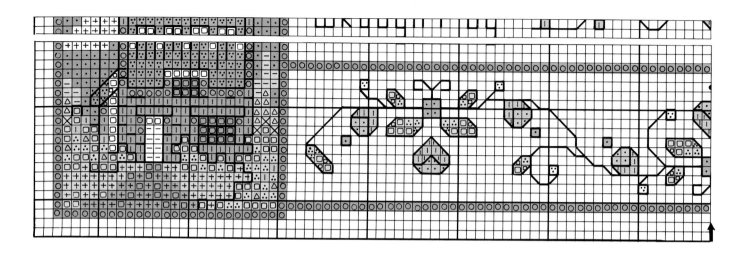

A Time to Share

Stitched on cream Linen 28 over 2 threads, the finished design size is 10⅜" x 13⅜". The fabric was cut 17" x 20".

FABRICS   **DESIGN SIZES**
Aida 11   13¼" x 17⅛"
Aida 14   10⅜" x 13⅜"
Aida 18   8⅛" x 10½"
Aida 22   6⅝" x 8½"

Anchor   **DMC (used for sample)**

Step 1: Cross-stitch (2 strands)

Anchor			DMC	
1	+			White
386			746	Off White
886			3047	Yellow Beige-lt.
301			744	Yellow-pale
4146			950	Peach Pecan-dk.
868			758	Terra Cotta-lt.
882	●		407	Pecan
49			963	Wild Rose-vy. lt.
75			3733	Dusty Rose-lt.
76			3731	Dusty Rose-med.
108			211	Lavender-lt.
105			209	Lavender-dk.
158			3756	Baby Blue-ultra vy. lt.
128	—		800	Delft-pale

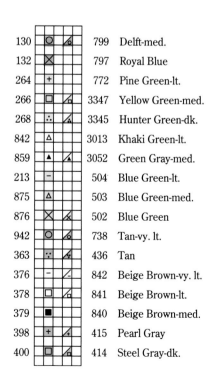

Anchor			DMC	
130			799	Delft-med.
132	X		797	Royal Blue
264	+		772	Pine Green-lt.
266			3347	Yellow Green-med.
268			3345	Hunter Green-dk.
842			3013	Khaki Green-lt.
859	▲		3052	Green Gray-med.
213	—		504	Blue Green-lt.
875			503	Blue Green-med.
876	X		502	Blue Green
942			738	Tan-vy. lt.
363			436	Tan
376	—		842	Beige Brown-vy. lt.
378			841	Beige Brown-lt.
379	■		840	Beige Brown-med.
398	+		415	Pearl Gray
400			414	Steel Gray-dk.

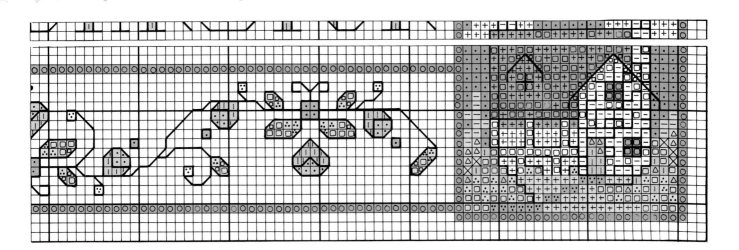

Step 2: Backstitch (1 strand)

76	3731	Dusty Rose-med. (pink flowers and window shutters, door on large house, name)
105	209	Lavender-dk. (lavender alphabet and flowers)
132	797	Royal Blue (poem, numbers, WROUGHT BY)
266	3347	Yellow Green-med. (green alphabet)
268	3345	Hunter Green-dk. (all greenery)

355	975	Golden Brown-dk. (all houses except roof on bottom right house, yellow flowers)
398	415	Pearl Gray (inside windows)
236	3799	Pewter Gray-vy. dk. (all else)

Step 3: French Knot (1 strand)

76	3731	Dusty Rose-med.
105	209	Lavender-dk.
355	975	Golden Brown-dk.

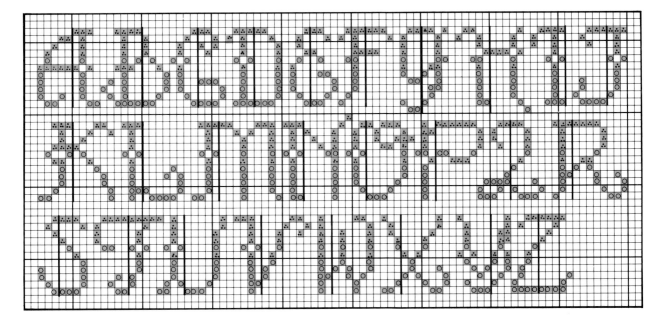

Alphabet for banners on pages 120-123.

Friendly Salutations

MATERIALS

One 9" x 12" piece of cream perforated paper
Completed design piece on cream Linen 28
1½ yards of ⅜"-wide blue flat trim
1½ yards of ⅛"-wide blue flat trim
9" x 9" piece of mat board
Acrylic paint: light blue
Sponge
Dressmaker's pen
Spray adhesive
Tacky glue

DIRECTIONS

1. Dilute light blue acrylic paint with water to the consistency of ink. Sponge-paint one side of the perforated paper. Let dry, then complete stitching.

2. With house motif centered, cut the fabric to 9" x 9". With welcome friends motif centered, cut the perforated paper to 9" x 9".

3. Place house motif flat with right side up. Center welcome friends motif, right side up, over house motif. Trace the oval outline of the house motif onto the perforated paper in the center of the welcome friends motif. Carefully cut oval shape from the perforated paper.

4. Coat the back of the perforated paper with spray adhesive. Align oval cutout over house motif. Press perforated paper onto linen. Coat mat board with spray adhesive. Align perforated paper/linen over mat board. Press onto mat board.

5. Glue ⅜"-wide trim around outside edges of perforated paper. To make hanger, cut one 16" length from remaining ⅜"-wide trim. Glue one end of trim to each top corner of perforated paper.

6. Glue ⅛"-wide trim ½" from edge of ⅜"-wide flat trim in a square around perforated paper. Glue remaining ⅛"-wide trim around oval on perforated paper. Cut excess.

117

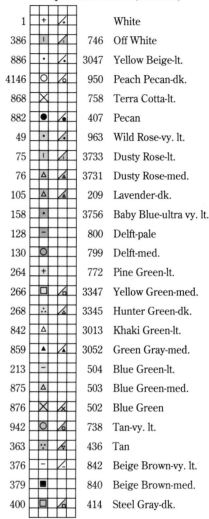

Anchor				DMC (used for sample)	
Step 1: Cross-stitch (2 strands)					
1	+	/			White
386	I	/		746	Off White
886	·	/		3047	Yellow Beige-lt.
4146	O	/		950	Peach Pecan-dk.
868	X			758	Terra Cotta-lt.
882	●	/		407	Pecan
49	·	/		963	Wild Rose-vy. lt.
75	I	/		3733	Dusty Rose-lt.
76	△	/		3731	Dusty Rose-med.
105	△	/		209	Lavender-dk.
158	·			3756	Baby Blue-ultra vy. lt.
128	–			800	Delft-pale
130	O			799	Delft-med.
264	+			772	Pine Green-lt.
266	□	/		3347	Yellow Green-med.
268	∴	/		3345	Hunter Green-dk.
842	△			3013	Khaki Green-lt.
859	▲	/		3052	Green Gray-med.
213	–			504	Blue Green-lt.
875	△			503	Blue Green-med.
876	X	/		502	Blue Green
942	O	/		738	Tan-vy. lt.
363	∴	/		436	Tan
376	–	/		842	Beige Brown-vy. lt.
379	■			840	Beige Brown-med.
400	□	/		414	Steel Gray-dk.

Step 2: Backstitch (1 strand)

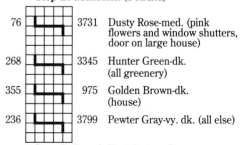

		DMC	
76		3731	Dusty Rose-med. (pink flowers and window shutters, door on large house)
268		3345	Hunter Green-dk. (all greenery)
355		975	Golden Brown-dk. (house)
236		3799	Pewter Gray-vy. dk. (all else)

Step 3: French Knot (1 strand)

76	■	3731	Dusty Rose-med.

Stitch Count: 79 x 89

Stitch Count: 74 x 51

Welcome Friends: Stitched on cream perforated paper, the finished design size is 5½" x 6¼". The paper was cut 11" x 11". Complete Step 1 before stitching.

House: Stitched on cream Linen 28 over 2 threads, the finished design size is 5¼" x 3⅝". The fabric was cut 12" x 10".

Heritage Banners

Stitched on cream Linen 28 over 2 threads, the finished design size for one banner is 4¼" x 4". The fabric for each banner was cut 8" x 10". See Step 1 for placement. To personalize your banners, replace these letters with desired letters from the alphabet on page 115.

MATERIALS (for one)

Completed design on cream Linen 28;
    matching thread
6" x 7" piece of white flannel
1¼ yards of ⅛"-wide blue cording; matching thread
5"-long ¼"-wide dowel
Liquid ravel preventer

Stitch Count: 60 x 56

DIRECTIONS
All seams are ¼".

1. Choose house design from the following pages. Begin stitching top edge of house design centered horizontally and 2¼" from top edge of fabric.

2. When the design is complete, cut linen to 6" x 14", centering the design horizontally. With right sides facing, fold linen in half and align side edges. Pin flannel to wrong side of front, matching edges. Stitch sides together, leaving the top open. Turn.

3. Fold the top raw edges 1" to the back of the banner. Fold raw edges under ¼" and hand-stitch in place to back side of banner. Insert dowel into casing.

4. Leaving 11" tail extending above corner, begin hand stitching cording around border at one top corner. Continue stitching cording around entire banner. End at opposite corner and trim excess to an 11" tail. Apply liquid ravel preventer to ends of cording. Tie ends of tails together to form hanging loop.

Stitch Count: 60 x 56

121

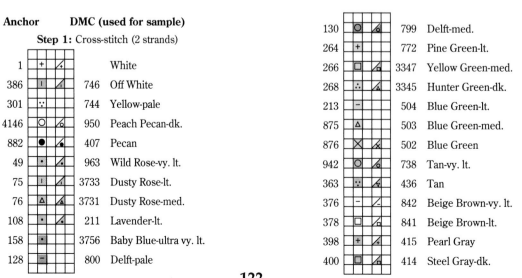

Anchor			DMC (used for sample)
		Step 1:	**Cross-stitch (2 strands)**
1	+	◢	White
386	I	◢	746 Off White
301	∴		744 Yellow-pale
4146	○	◢	950 Peach Pecan-dk.
882	●	◢	407 Pecan
49	·	◢	963 Wild Rose-vy. lt.
75	I	◢	3733 Dusty Rose-lt.
76	△	◢	3731 Dusty Rose-med.
108	·	◢	211 Lavender-lt.
158	·		3756 Baby Blue-ultra vy. lt.
128	–		800 Delft-pale

130	○	◢	799 Delft-med.
264	+		772 Pine Green-lt.
266	□	◢	3347 Yellow Green-med.
268	∴	◢	3345 Hunter Green-dk.
213	–		504 Blue Green-lt.
875	△		503 Blue Green-med.
876	✕	◢	502 Blue Green
942	○	◢	738 Tan-vy. lt.
363	∴	◢	436 Tan
376	–	◢	842 Beige Brown-vy. lt.
378	□	◢	841 Beige Brown-lt.
398	+	◢	415 Pearl Gray
400	□	◢	414 Steel Gray-dk.

122

Stitch Count: 60 x 56

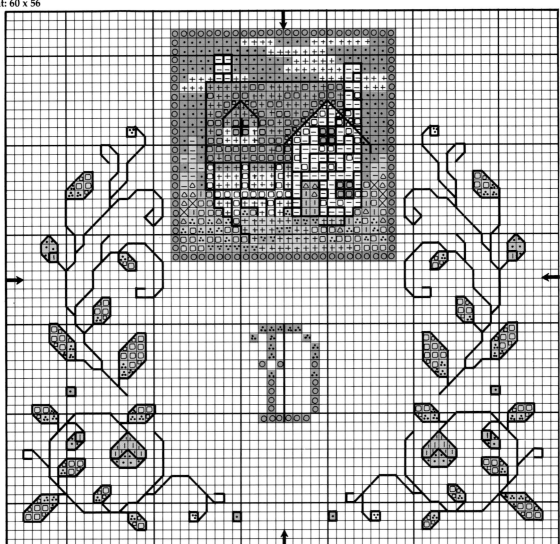

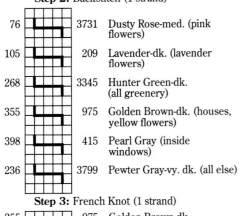

Step 2: Backstitch (1 strand)

76	3731	Dusty Rose-med. (pink flowers)
105	209	Lavender-dk. (lavender flowers)
268	3345	Hunter Green-dk. (all greenery)
355	975	Golden Brown-dk. (houses, yellow flowers)
398	415	Pearl Gray (inside windows)
236	3799	Pewter Gray-vy. dk. (all else)

Step 3: French Knot (1 strand)

355	975	Golden Brown-dk.

Banner alphabet on page 115.

Anchor	DMC (used for sample)

Step 1: Cross-stitch (2 strands)

130	799	Delft-med.
132	797	Royal Blue

Step 2: Backstitch (1 strand)

132	797	Royal Blue

123

*If it is
given with
love,
a mere
handful is
enough.*

—

Unknown

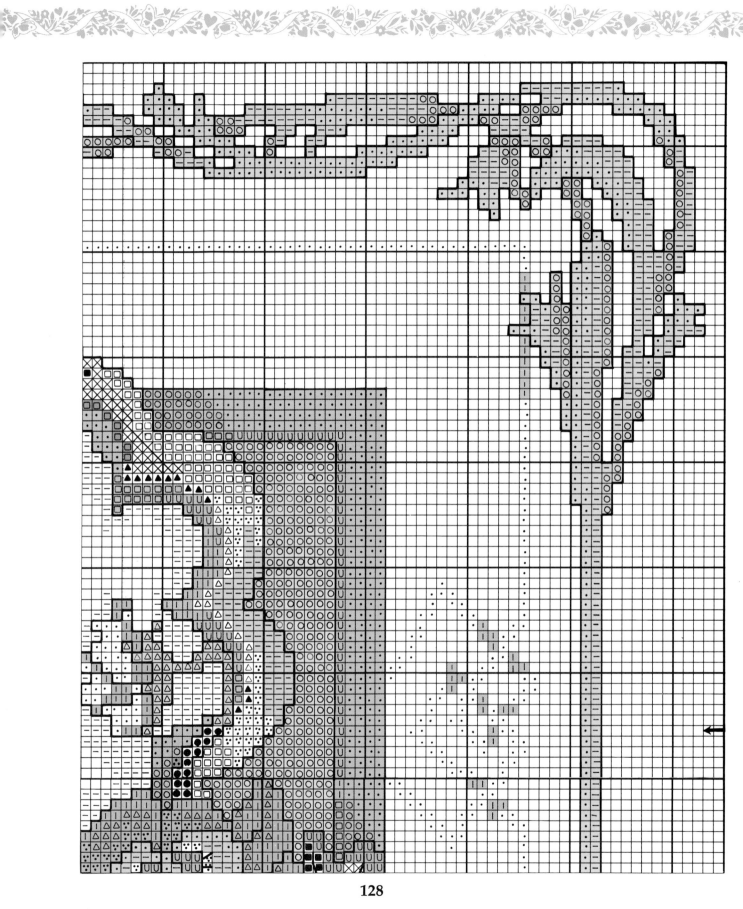

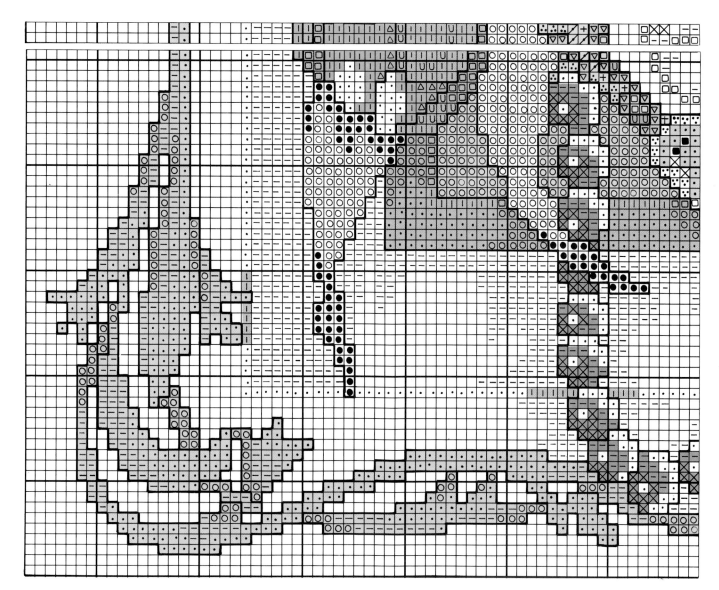

Tokens of Affection

Stitched on tea-dyed Linen 28 over 2 threads, the finished design size is 13⅜" x 8¾". The fabric was cut 20" x 15".

FABRICS	**DESIGN SIZES**
Aida 11	17⅛" x 11⅛"
Aida 14	13⅜" x 8¾"
Aida 18	10½" x 6⅞"
Hardanger 22	8½" x 5⅝"

Anchor   **DMC (used for sample)**
Step 1: Cross-stitch (2 strands)

Anchor		DMC	
1	·		White
386	╱	746	Off White
292	·	3078	Golden Yellow-vy. lt.
301	─	744	Yellow-pale
306	∴	725	Topaz

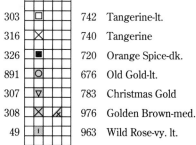

Anchor		DMC	
303	□	742	Tangerine-lt.
316	✕	740	Tangerine
326	■	720	Orange Spice-dk.
891	○	676	Old Gold-lt.
307	▽	783	Christmas Gold
308	✕ ╱	976	Golden Brown-med.
49	I	963	Wild Rose-vy. lt.

129

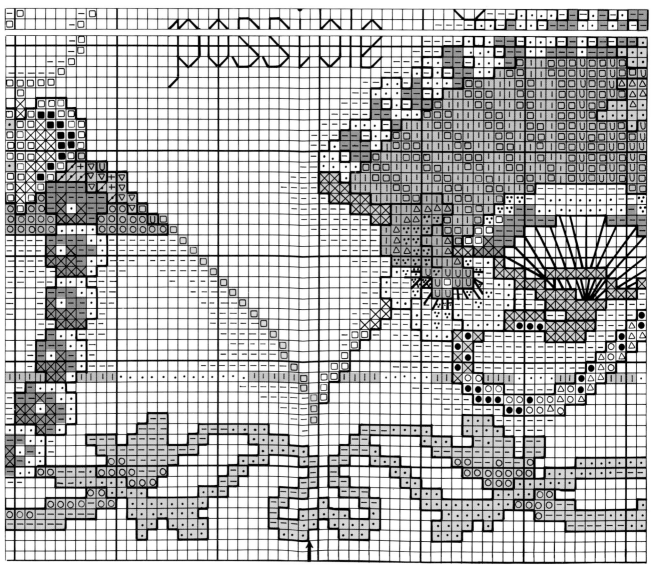

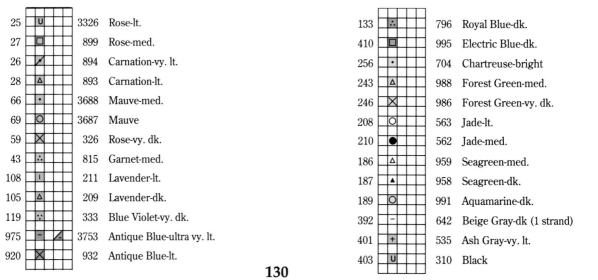

25	U	3326	Rose-lt.		
27	□	899	Rose-med.		
26	╱	894	Carnation-vy. lt.		
28	△	893	Carnation-lt.		
66	·	3688	Mauve-med.		
69	○	3687	Mauve		
59	✕	326	Rose-vy. dk.		
43	∴	815	Garnet-med.		
108	I	211	Lavender-lt.		
105	△	209	Lavender-dk.		
119	∴	333	Blue Violet-vy. dk.		
975	— ╱	3753	Antique Blue-ultra vy. lt.		
920	✕	932	Antique Blue-lt.		

133	∴	796	Royal Blue-dk.		
410	□	995	Electric Blue-dk.		
256	·	704	Chartreuse-bright		
243	△	988	Forest Green-med.		
246	✕	986	Forest Green-vy. dk.		
208	○	563	Jade-lt.		
210	●	562	Jade-med.		
186	△	959	Seagreen-med.		
187	▲	958	Seagreen-dk.		
189	○	991	Aquamarine-dk.		
392	—	642	Beige Gray-dk (1 strand)		
401	+	535	Ash Gray-vy. lt.		
403	U	310	Black		

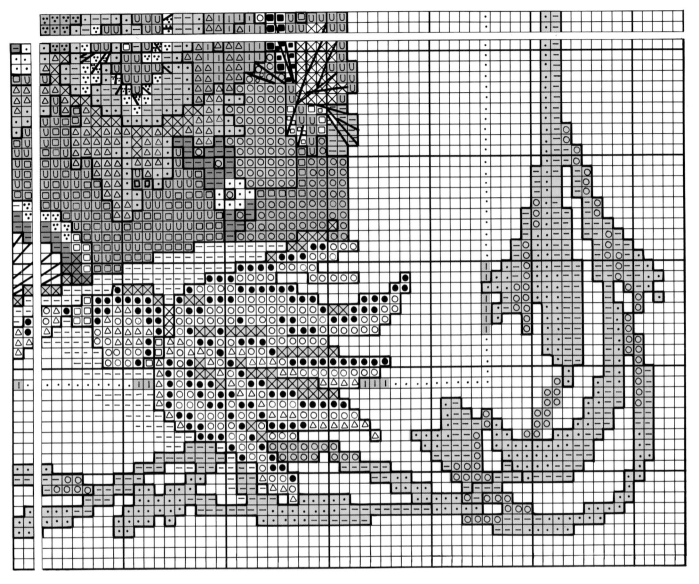

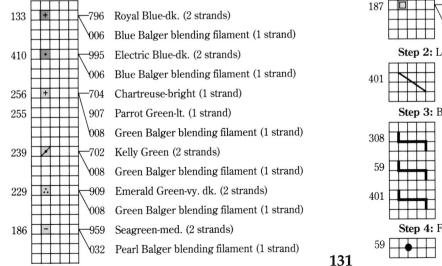

133   796   Royal Blue-dk. (2 strands)
     006   Blue Balger blending filament (1 strand)

410   995   Electric Blue-dk. (2 strands)
     006   Blue Balger blending filament (1 strand)

256   704   Chartreuse-bright (1 strand)

255   907   Parrot Green-lt. (1 strand)
     008   Green Balger blending filament (1 strand)

239   702   Kelly Green (2 strands)
     008   Green Balger blending filament (1 strand)

229   909   Emerald Green-vy. dk. (2 strands)
     008   Green Balger blending filament (1 strand)

186   959   Seagreen-med. (2 strands)
     032   Pearl Balger blending filament (1 strand)

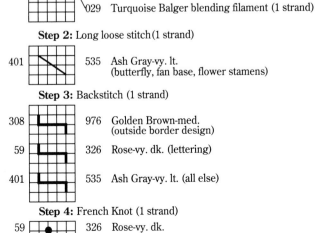

187   958   Seagreen-dk. (2 strands)
     029   Turquoise Balger blending filament (1 strand)

Step 2: Long loose stitch (1 strand)

401   535   Ash Gray-vy. lt.
             (butterfly, fan base, flower stamens)

Step 3: Backstitch (1 strand)

308   976   Golden Brown-med.
             (outside border design)

59   326   Rose-vy. dk. (lettering)

401   535   Ash Gray-vy. lt. (all else)

Step 4: French Knot (1 strand)

59   326   Rose-vy. dk.

131

Velvety Christmas Wishes

MATERIALS

Completed design piece on ruby-red Linen 28;
matching thread
⅜ yard of unstitched ruby-red Linen 28
⅝ yard of burgundy cotton fabric
1 yard of burgundy velvet
⅝ yard of black lightweight fusible interfacing
Fleece
2 yards of medium cording

DIRECTIONS
All seams are ¼".

1. Enlarge pattern for stocking on page 136. With design centered and 5" below top edge, cut one stocking front. From unstitched linen, cut one stocking back. From interfacing, cut two stocking pieces. Fuse, following manufacturer's instructions, to wrong sides of linen pieces. From cotton fabric, cut two stocking pieces for liner. From fleece, cut two stocking pieces. From velvet, cut two 7" x 45" strips for cuff , two 9½" x 3¼" strips for lining and one 4" x 2" strip for hanger. From remaining velvet, cut 1¼"-wide bias strips, piecing to equal 2 yards. Make 2 yards of corded piping.

2. Stitch the two 7" x 45" velvet strips end-to-end to make one strip 90" long. Sew gathering stitches along both long sides of strip. Gather top and bottom tightly. Set aside.

3. Beginning and ending ¾" from stocking top, stitch piping around edge of stocking front.

4. Baste one fleece stocking to wrong side of stocking front and one fleece stocking to wrong side of stocking back. Then stitch stocking front and back together with right sides facing, sewing on stitching line of piping. Trim fleece from seam allowances. Clip curves; turn.

5. Draw a horizontal line 4¾" from top edge across stocking front and back. Lay raw edge of gathered strip, wrong side up, along the line. Beginning at center back, stitch gathered piece to stocking along line, ending 2" from center back. Cut excess fabric. Align raw ends of gathered piece. Stitch raw ends together. Finish stitching across center back of stocking; see Diagram A.

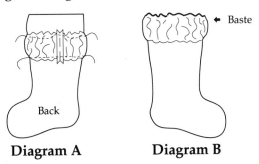

Diagram A   **Diagram B**

6. Flip gathered piece up and align raw edge with top of stocking. Baste top edges together; see Diagram B.

7. To make hanger, fold 4" x 2" velvet piece in half with right sides facing so that it measures 1" wide. Stitch long edges together. Turn. With seam in center back, fold in half to form a loop. Pin ends to top left edge of stocking. Stitch in place.

8. Align long edge of one 9½" x 3¼" velvet strip with top of each lining piece; see Diagram C. With right sides facing, stitch velvet strip to lining. With right sides facing, stitch lining front to back, leaving top open and an opening in heel seam. Do not turn. Slide lining over stocking with right sides facing, side seams matching and hanger at top sandwiched between. Stitch around top edge of stocking through all layers. Turn stocking through opening in lining. Slipstitch opening closed. Tuck lining inside stocking.

Diagram C

Stitched on ruby-red Linen 28 over 2
threads, the finished design size is 6⅝" x 7".
The fabric was cut 15" x 20".

FABRICS	DESIGN SIZES
Aida 11	8½" x 8⅞"
Aida 14	6⅝" x 7"
Aida 18	5⅛" x 5⅜"
Hardanger 22	4¼" x 4½"

Anchor   DMC (used for sample)
Step 1: Cross-stitch (2 strands)

Anchor		DMC	
1	·		White
386	╱	746	Off White
292	•	3078	Golden Yellow-vy. lt.
301	−	744	Yellow-pale
306	∷	725	Topaz
303	□	742	Tangerine-lt.
316	✕	740	Tangerine
326	■	720	Orange Spice-dk.
307	▽	783	Christmas Gold
308	✕ ╱	976	Golden Brown-med.
49	ı	963	Wild Rose-vy. lt.
25	U	3326	Rose-lt.
27	□	899	Rose-med.
26	╱	894	Carnation-vy. lt.
28	△	893	Carnation-lt.
59	✕	326	Rose-vy. dk.
43	∴	815	Garnet-med.
108	ı	211	Lavender-lt.
105	△	209	Lavender-dk.

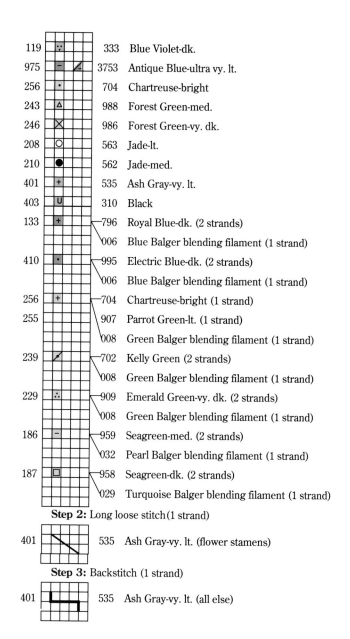

Anchor		DMC	
119	∷	333	Blue Violet-dk.
975	− ╱	3753	Antique Blue-ultra vy. lt.
256	·	704	Chartreuse-bright
243	△	988	Forest Green-med.
246	✕	986	Forest Green-vy. dk.
208	○	563	Jade-lt.
210	●	562	Jade-med.
401	+	535	Ash Gray-vy. lt.
403	U	310	Black
133	+	796	Royal Blue-dk. (2 strands)
		006	Blue Balger blending filament (1 strand)
410	•	995	Electric Blue-dk. (2 strands)
		006	Blue Balger blending filament (1 strand)
256	+	704	Chartreuse-bright (1 strand)
255		907	Parrot Green-lt. (1 strand)
		008	Green Balger blending filament (1 strand)
239	╱	702	Kelly Green (2 strands)
		008	Green Balger blending filament (1 strand)
229	∴	909	Emerald Green-vy. dk. (2 strands)
		008	Green Balger blending filament (1 strand)
186	−	959	Seagreen-med. (2 strands)
		032	Pearl Balger blending filament (1 strand)
187	□	958	Seagreen-dk. (2 strands)
		029	Turquoise Balger blending filament (1 strand)

Step 2: Long loose stitch (1 strand)

401		535	Ash Gray-vy. lt. (flower stamens)

Step 3: Backstitch (1 strand)

401		535	Ash Gray-vy. lt. (all else)

Stitch Count: 93 x 98

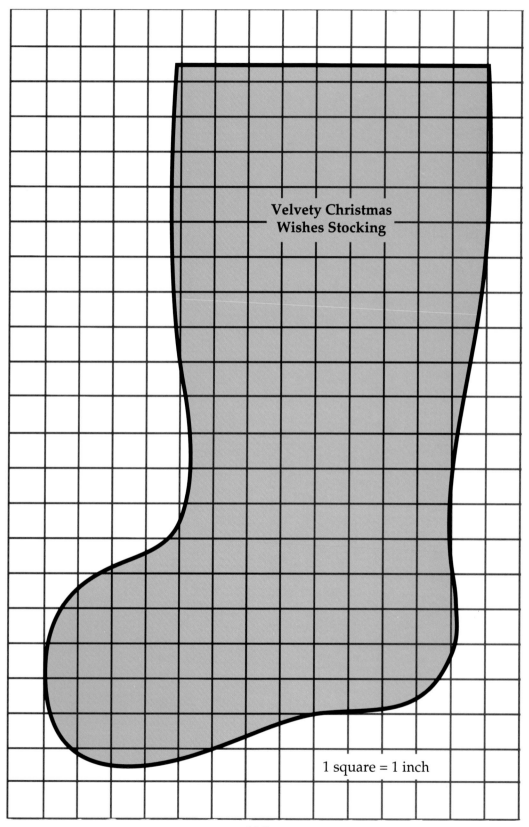

Velvety Christmas Wishes Stocking

1 square = 1 inch

Pins of Preference

Stitched on tea-dyed Linen 28 over 2 threads, the finished design size is 3¼" x 2⅞". The fabric was cut 15" x 15".

FABRICS	DESIGN SIZES
Aida 11	4⅛" x 3¾"
Aida 14	3¼" x 2⅞"
Aida 18	2½" x 2¼"
Hardanger 22	2⅛" x 1⅞"

MATERIALS

Completed design piece on tea-dyed Linen 28; matching thread
8"-wide circle of green moiré fabric
One 4½"-wide clay flowerpot saucer
1 yard of ½"-wide gathered light green trim
Three ½"-wide brass beads
Polyester stuffing
Hot glue gun and glue sticks
Pins

DIRECTIONS

1. With design centered, cut fabric into a 14" circle. Zigzag edges of both circle pieces. Stitch a gathering thread around outer edge of fabric; gather loosely.

2. Stuff center of design piece firmly. Tighten gathering thread, forming a pincushion to fit inside saucer. Secure thread.

3. With right side up, place saucer in center of wrong side of moiré fabric. Gather fabric around saucer, gluing fabric edges inside saucer.

4. Center and glue base of pincushion inside saucer. Cut trim in half. Crisscross lengths around base of pincushion using pins to hold in place. Glue. Remove pins.

5. Turn pincushion upside down. For feet, glue beads to fabric about 2" apart on bottom of saucer, forming a triangle.

Stitch Count: 46 x 41

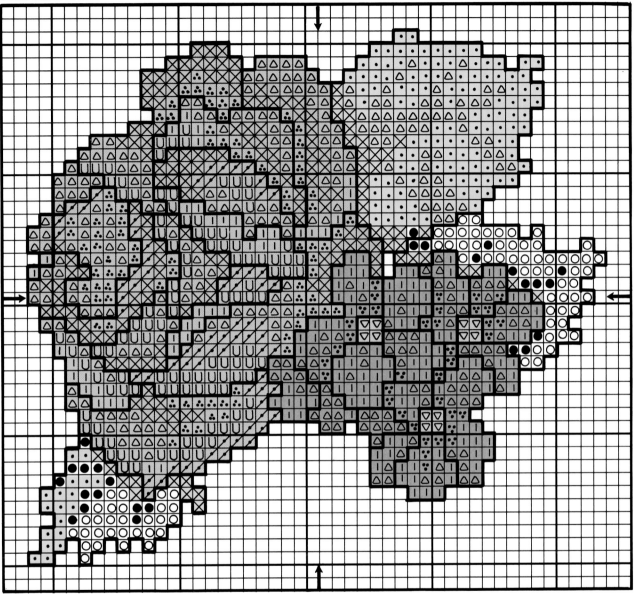

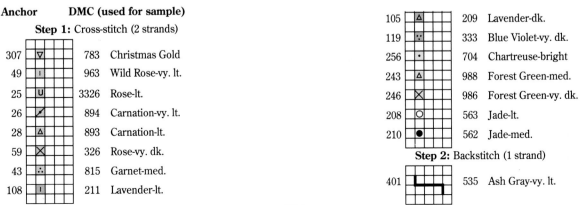

Anchor   **DMC (used for sample)**

Step 1: Cross-stitch (2 strands)

307	▽	783 Christmas Gold
49	I	963 Wild Rose-vy. lt.
25	U	3326 Rose-lt.
26	/	894 Carnation-vy. lt.
28	△	893 Carnation-lt.
59	✕	326 Rose-vy. dk.
43	∴	815 Garnet-med.
108	I	211 Lavender-lt.

105	△	209 Lavender-dk.
119	∷	333 Blue Violet-vy. dk.
256	•	704 Chartreuse-bright
243	△	988 Forest Green-med.
246	✕	986 Forest Green-vy. dk.
208	○	563 Jade-lt.
210	●	562 Jade-med.

Step 2: Backstitch (1 strand)

401	⌐	535 Ash Gray-vy. lt.

139

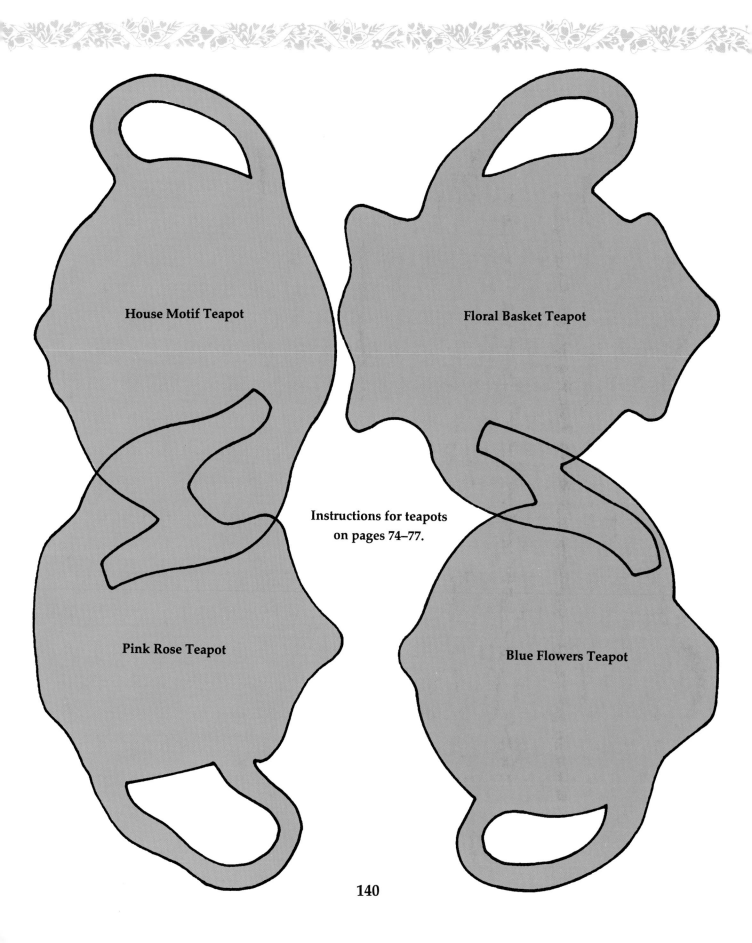

House Motif Teapot

Floral Basket Teapot

Instructions for teapots
on pages 74–77.

Pink Rose Teapot

Blue Flowers Teapot

Cross-Stitch

Fabrics: Counted cross-stitch is usually worked on even-weave fabric. These fabrics are manufactured specifically for counted thread embroidery and are woven with the same number of vertical as horizontal threads per inch. Because the number of threads in the fabric is equal in each direction, each stitch will be the same size. It is the number of threads per inch in even-weave fabrics that determines the size of a finished design.

Waste Canvas: Waste canvas is a coarse, fabric-like substance used as a guide for cross-stitching on fabrics other than even-weaves. Cut the waste canvas 1" larger on all sides than the finished design size. Baste it to the fabric to be stitched. Complete the stitching. Then, dampen the stitched area with cold water. Pull the waste canvas threads out one at a time with tweezers. It is easier to pull all the threads running in one direction first, then pull out the opposite threads. Allow the stitching to dry. Place face down on a towel and iron.

Preparing Fabric: Cut even-weave fabric at least 3" larger on all sides than the design size, or cut it the size specified in the instructions. If the item is to be finished into a pillow, for example, the fabric should be cut as directed. A 3" margin is the minimum amount of space that allows for comfortably working the edges of the design. To prevent fraying, whipstitch or machine zigzag raw fabric edges.

Needles: Needles should slip easily through the holes in the fabric but not pierce the fabric. Use a blunt tapestry needle, size 24 or 26. Never leave the needle in the design area of your work. It can leave rust or a permanent impression on the fabric.

Floss: All numbers and color names are cross-referenced between Anchor and DMC brands of floss. Run the floss over a damp sponge to straighten. Separate all six strands and use the number of strands called for in the code.

Centering the Design: Fold the fabric in half horizontally, then vertically. Place a pin in the fold point to mark the center. Locate the center of the design on the graph by following the vertical and horizontal arrows in the left and bottom margins. Begin stitching all designs at the center point of the graph and the fabric unless the instructions indicate otherwise.

Graphs: Each symbol represents a different color. Make one stitch for each symbol, referring to the code to verify which stitch to use. Use the small arrows in the margins to find the center of the graph. When a graph is continued, the bottom two rows of the graph on the previous page are repeated, separated by a small space, indicating where to connect them. The stitch count is printed with each graph, listing first the width, then the length of the design.

Codes: The code indicates the brand of thread used to stitch the model, as well as the cross-reference for using another brand. The steps in the code identify the stitch to be used and the number of floss strands for that stitch. The symbols match the graph, and give the color number and name for the thread. A symbol under a diagonal line indicates a half cross-stitch. Blended threads are represented on the code and graph with a single symbol, but both color names are listed.

Securing the Floss: Insert your needle up from the underside of the fabric at your starting point. Hold 1" of thread behind the fabric and stitch over it, securing with the first few stitches. To finish thread, run under four or more stitches on the back of the design. Never knot floss unless working on clothing. Another method of securing floss is the waste knot. Knot your floss and insert your needle from the right side of the fabric about 1" inside the design area. Work several stitches over the thread to secure. Cut off the knot later.

141

Stitching: For a smooth cross-stitch, use the "push and pull" method. Push the needle straight down and-completely through fabric before pulling. Do not pull the thread tightly. Consistent tension throughout ensures even stitches. Make one stitch for every symbol on the chart. To stitch in rows, work from left to right and then back. Half-crosses are used to make a rounded shape. Make the longer stitch in the direction of the slanted line.

Carrying Floss: To carry floss, weave floss under the previously worked stitches on the back. Do not carry thread across any fabric that is not or will not be stitched. Loose threads, especially dark ones, will show through the fabric.

Twisted Floss: If floss is twisted, drop the needle and allow the floss to unwind itself. Floss will cover best when lying flat. Use thread no longer than 18" because it will tend to twist and knot.

Cleaning Completed Work: When stitching is complete, soak it in cold water with a mild soap for five to ten minutes. Rinse well and roll in a towel to remove excess water. Do not wring. Place work face down on a dry towel and iron on a warm setting until dry.

Cross-stitch: Make one cross for each symbol on the chart. Bring needle and thread up at A, down at B, up at C, and down again at D. For rows, stitch from left to right, then back. All stitches should lie in the same direction.

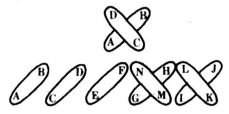

Half Cross-stitch: The stitch actually fits three-fourths of the area. Make the longer stitch in the direction of the slanted line on the graph. Bring needle and thread up at A, down at B, up at C, and down at D.

Backstitch: Complete all cross-stitching before working backstitches or other accent stitches. Working from left to right with one strand of floss (unless designated otherwise on code), bring needle and thread up at A, down at B, and up again at C. Go back down at A and continue in this manner.

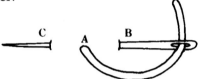

French Knot: Bring needle up at A, using one strand of embroidery floss. Wrap floss around needle two times (unless indicated otherwise in instructions). Insert needle beside A, pulling floss until it fits snugly around needle. Pull needle through to back.

Ladder Hemstitch: Determine approximate center of area to be hemstitched. Using sharp embroidery scissors, carefully cut horizontal threads only at center point. With needle, draw cut horizontal threads to sides of fabric, leaving free exact number of vertical threads needed for hemstitching.

At ends of drawn area, thread needle with drawn horizontal threads and reweave them 1" into wrong side of fabric. Trim threads.

To secure hem, fold hem to back of fabric so that edge of hem lies just below bottom edge of drawn area. Baste hem in place. When working hemstitching, be sure that stitches catch folded edge of hem.

Begin with a waste knot, knotting end of thread and bringing needle up 1" from where hemstitching will begin. Place knot so that first four stitches will cover the 1" length of thread on wrong side. After working first stitches, cut off knot. When hemstitching is completed, weave thread under last four stitches on wrong side.

On right side of fabric, work stitches from left to right. Bring needle up from wrong side of fabric. Slip needle from right to left under four vertical threads and bring to right side. Pass needle from left to right over same four threads, insert needle from right to wrong to right side of fabric at point just left of encircled threads. Pull stitch tightly to make cluster. Continue in clusters of four threads each along drawn area. At end, invert fabric, and work hem-stitch along opposite edge, grouping same threads as were grouped before to form a ladder like pattern.

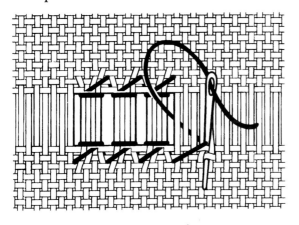

Sewing Hints

Patterns: Use tracing paper to trace patterns. Be sure to transfer all information. All patterns include seam allowances. The seam allowance is ¼" unless otherwise specified.

Marking on Fabric: Always use a dressmaker's pen or chalk to mark on fabric. It will wash out when you clean your finished piece.

Gathering: Machine-stitch two parallel rows of long stitches ¼" and ½" from the edge of the fabric (unless indicated otherwise in instructions). Leave the ends of the thread 2" or 3" long. Pull the two bobbin threads and gather to fit the desired length. Long edges may need to be gathered from both ends. Disperse the fullness evenly and secure the threads in the area by wrapping them around a pin in a figure eight.

Slipstitch: Insert needle at A, taking a small stitch, and slide it through the folded edge of the fabric about ⅛" to ¼", bringing it out at B.

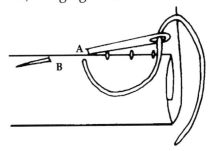

Enlarging a Pattern: On a sheet of paper large enough to hold the finished pattern, mark grid lines 1" apart to fill the paper. Begin marking dots on 1" grid lines where the reduced pattern intersects the corresponding grid line. Connect the dots. Fabric stores sell pattern-making products that can save a great deal of time.

Bias Strips: Bias strips are used for ruffles, binding or corded piping. To cut bias, fold the fabric at a 45-degree angle to the grain of the fabric and crease. Cut on the crease. Cut additional strips the width indicated in the instructions and parallel to the first cutting line. The ends of the bias strips should be on the grain of the fabric. Place the right sides of the ends together and stitch with a ¼" seam. Continue to piece the strips until they are the length that is indicated in the instructions.

Corded Piping: Center cording on the wrong side of the bias strip and fold the fabric over it, aligning raw edges. Using a zipper foot, stitch through both layers of fabric close to the cording. Trim the seam allowance to ¼".

Suppliers

Aida 14 (white)
Murano 30 (cream)
Quaker Cloth 28 (driftwood)
Waste Canvas 14
Zweigart/Joan Toggit Ltd.
35 Fairfield Place
West Caldwell NJ 07006

Aida 14 (white)
Linen 28 (cream, natural, tea-dyed, white)
Estate Towel (white)
Charles Craft
P.O. Box 1049
Laurinburg NC 28352

Linen 28 (amber, ruby-red)
Wichelt
Route 1 Hwy 35
Stoddard WI 54658

Hemstitched Border Linen band (natural)
Potpourri Etc.
209 Richmond Street
El Segundo CA 90245

Balger Blending Filament
Kreinik Mfg. Co., Inc.
P.O. Box 1966
Pakersburg WV 26102

Batting, fleece, polyester stuffing
Fairfield Processing Corporation
88 Rose Hill Avenue
P.O. Drawer 1157
Danbury CT 06819

Sewing Machine
Bernina of America
534 W. Chestnut
Hinsdale IL 60521

Glue
Aleene's
85 Industrial Way
Buellton CA 93427

Teapot Die-cuts
Chapelle Designers
P.O. Box 9252
Ogden UT 84409

Ribbon
Offray & Son, Inc.
Route 24 Box 601
Chester NJ 07930

Perforated Paper
Will Maur Crafts
735 Old York Road
Willow Grove PA 19090

Index

All of us at Meredith® Press are dedicated to offering you, our customer, the best books we can create. We are particularly concerned that all of the instructions for making projects are clear and accurate. Please address your correspondence to Customer Service Department, Meredith® Press, Meredith Corporation, 150 East 52nd Street, New York, NY 10022.

Gifts of Love: An American Sampler is the sixth in a series of cross-stitch books. If you would like the first five books in the series, *Quilt Designs in Cross-Stitch: An American Sampler 1989, Country Cross-Stitch Designs: An American Sampler 1990, Home Is Where the Heart Is: An American Sampler 1991, The Changing Seasons: An American Sampler 1992, and In My Mother's Garden: An American Sampler 1993*, Please write to Better Homes and Gardens Books, P.O. Box 10670, Des Moines, IA 50336, or call 1-800-678-2665.

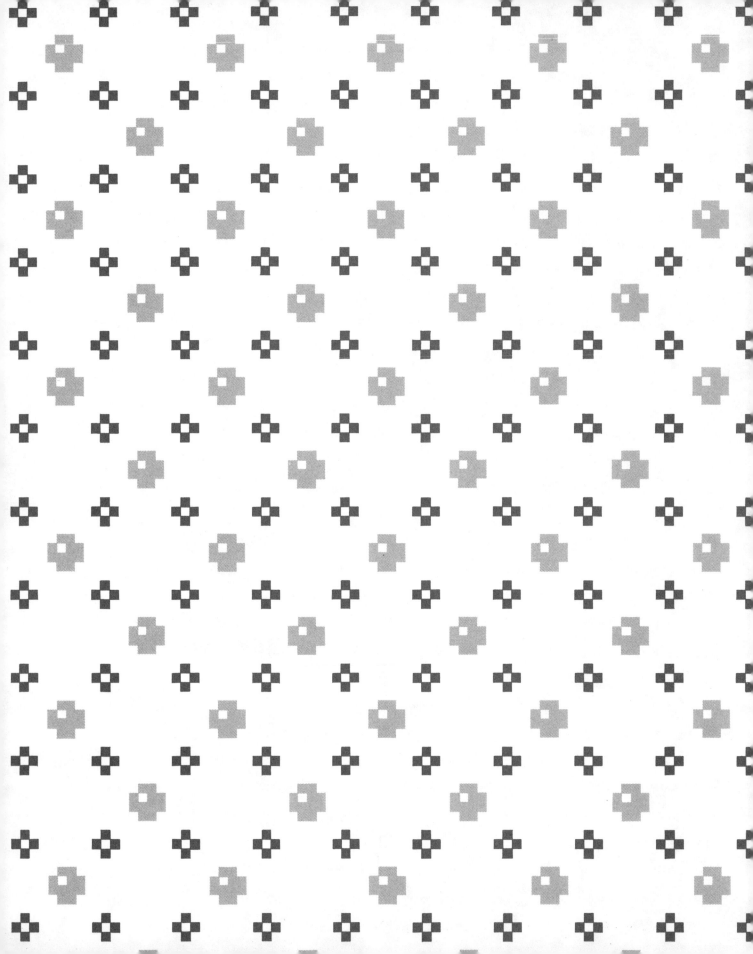